ADVANCE PRAISE

"Most of us will never run an ultra, mere mortals that we are. Michele Graglia's inspiring and engrossing book helps us understand the 'why' and that the boundaries are only there to be pushed. His pivot from supermodel to his first failed race to becoming one of the best ultra athletes and finding his spots in the Guinness World Record book is a remarkable one. Ultra traces this personal journey through inspiring quotes and fascinating and emotional stories from his races. But it's a lot more than that. It's the chronicle of one exceptional athlete, who has lived so many diverse lives in his young years, connecting with nature, transcending himself, and, along the way, encouraging all of us to discover our own true strength and resilience.

This is a great read for anyone considering athletic challenges or in search of some greater personal goal. There is no telling where this book might take you."

—JULIE CHRISCO ANDREWS, TWENTY-FIVE-YEAR, FIVE-TIME EMMY-WINNING SPORTS PRODUCER, NBC SPORTS & ESPN

"A revealing and unexpected plot twist of what compelled an international top model to ditch the limelight and jet-setting lifestyle of high fashion to pursue a life of self-discovery at the frontiers of human endurance."

—DEAN KARNAZES, ULTRAMARATHON
LEGEND AND BEST-SELLING AUTHOR

"A riveting life story in pursuit of both outer and inner exploration."
—ANTON KRUPICKA, ULTRA TRAIL RUNNING ICON

"Ultra is an incredible story of hope, will, and perseverance."
—ADHARANAND FINN, AWARD-WINNING, BEST-SELLING AUTHOR

"An honest and compelling story that offers a true insight into the life journey of one of the most extreme ultra runners on the planet. Anyone interested in endurance, mindset, or accomplishing BIG goals needs to read this book."

—JESSE ITZLER, ENTREPRENEUR, AUTHOR, ENDURANCE
ATHLETE, AND PART-OWNER OF THE ATLANTA HAWKS

"Michele Graglia is a phenomenal athlete who exemplifies the possibility and urgency of changing your direction in life—even if it means rejecting fame and fortune—to pursue your passion and genuine calling. His story will inspire anyone who wants to break their mold and push their limits. Having spent time at races with Michele and seeing him win a grueling multi-day desert ultra, I am struck by his endearing combination of exceptional talent

and sincere humility. He truly is special but thankfully, doesn't act that way."

—SARAH LAVENDER SMITH, ULTRA RUNNING COACH AND AUTHOR OF *THE TRAIL RUNNER'S COMPANION: A STEP-BY-STEP GUIDE TO TRAIL RUNNING AND RACING, FROM 5KS TO ULTRAS*

"Inspiring. Michele sets a high example for many. A man who consciously decided to abandon the glamorous world of high fashion to pursue and then dedicate himself to one of the toughest disciplines in the world. To know him is an honor that makes me very proud."

—MARCO OLMO, TWO-TIME UTMB WINNER, AUTHOR, AND ULTRA TRAIL LEGEND

"Michele Graglia has written a book that holds nothing back. His unlikely path to ultra running fame left me in awe of his spirit and determination. His story proves that if we can just keep exploring the hidden corners of our existence, we can find parts of ourselves that we never imagined. Michele reminded me that every experience in life has value if we give our whole heart to it. When I finished reading this book, I immediately put on my running shoes and sprinted out the door for some miles because I needed to figure out what was next in my own life."

—CHARLIE ENGLE, ULTRA RUNNER, ADVENTURER, AND AUTHOR

"It is often said that running is a clear metaphor for life. In his very own way, Michele has made running the element capable of guiding him into a completely new dimension. If endurance is a *sport dominated by fatigue, sacrifice, and dedication, the stories contained in these pages, some raw and others compelling, show that for him, running was first of all the way to change the direction of his life and ultimately regain his inner freedom."*

—ROSARIO PALAZZOLO, *RUNNER'S WORLD*

ULTRA

TOP MODEL TO TOP ULTRA RUNNER

MICHELE GRAGLIA

WITH FOLCO TERZANI

HOUNDSTOOTH
PRESS

ULTRA
Top Model to Top Ultra Runner

ISBN   978-1-5445-2117-6 *Hardcover*
       978-1-5445-2116-9 *Paperback*
       978-1-5445-2115-2 *Ebook*

This book is dedicated to my parents, Cesare and Donatella,
who always encouraged me to follow my heart.

CONTENTS

INTRODUCTION

—FOLCO TERZANI, FLORENCE 2017

IT WAS AT THE END OF A RACE IN THE ALPS WHEN I FIRST saw him. He'd been lying on the grass for a while already, catching some rays, by the time I came in. A friend of mine whispered, "That guy's a world-class ultra runner."

"Ugh, too good-looking," I thought, and following an old prejudice, I assumed he must be dumb as well. So, that day we didn't even say hello.

A few months later, I met Michele in California and invited him to dinner with my family. He'd just come back from a horrendous race in the Yukon—one hundred miles through freezing mid-winter snows. He'd won the race. But I was even more astonished to discover that before becoming a runner, he'd been living the life of a top model in New York.

From hedonism, he'd moved to ultra running, a discipline

so demanding, with its quest for extreme distances, terrains, and pushing our physical and mental limits, that it's almost not a sport at all. He reminded me rather of certain characters I'd met during my childhood in Asia, like the abbot of the Shaolin monastery in China or the fakirs sitting on their beds of nails in India.

With the lucidity and extreme dedication that distinguish him, he'd run from a life of pleasures, luxury, and vices in the total opposite direction. Why?!

This is a recollection of our conversations. This is his story.

1.

PROMISE YOU'LL NEVER DO THAT AGAIN!

Everything that happened after simply followed. Because once you've found your path and you follow it, then you plow ahead, body and soul.

I'd never run a long race. "Five months of 'training' ought to do, right? I'm in great shape—what could possibly go wrong?" So, on May 13, I set off for the Keys 100. Those Keys were about to open the door of a whole new world to me. But first, I'd have to face the one-hundred-mile race I committed to, practically four marathons back to back—to back to back.

The Florida Keys are an extraordinary place—a group of little islands that form the shape of a comma from the south of

Florida down toward Cuba. There are bridges connecting one island to the next. To the left, you have the Atlantic Ocean, and to the right, in a different shade of blue, the Gulf of Mexico. You run on this road across the ocean, between coral reefs and mangroves, starting from Key Largo, which is one of the bigger islands, all the way to Key West. It's pretty spectacular.

My family: my mom, my dad, my sister, and my girlfriend, Lauren, came along to support me.

So, I show up at the starting line and see all these champions there. I recognize Pam Reed right away. She's a legend in the sport. In 2002, she'd even won the Badwater Ultra, which is considered one of the toughest foot races in the world. It's run across Death Valley in California right in the middle of summer, when it's hotter than anywhere else on the planet. And Pam didn't just come in first for the women—she came in first *overall*. She beat the fastest man by several hours!

Seeing her there now, a little off to the side, you wouldn't have given her the time of day. She was a tiny thing, about five-foot three, skinny, and light as a feather with short-cropped platinum hair, a sunburned face, and legs popping out of a white XL T-shirt. But when it comes to ultras, you can never judge a book by its cover. That's part of the beauty of this challenge.

At the Olympic Games, you never see a woman run faster than the men. But look beyond the conventional track-and-field conception of sports, where distances stretch till they become virtually impossible. Then, not just the gap between women and men starts to disappear, but even the gap between young and old. The reason is simple: it becomes less a question of the body and more of the mind. And according to Pam, women have a natural predisposition for ultras because they give birth and they know better how to deal with pain.

Marco Olmo, a tall, wiry, slightly lopsided guy who used to work as a truck driver at a cement factory in Italy, won the most prestigious trail race in the world in 2006, the Ultra Trail du Mont Blanc. He won it again the following year, for good measure. He was almost sixty years old.

These demonstrations are so impressive, they shake our very idea of human limits.

Now here I am, twenty-seven years old, still young, standing at the starting line of this ultra challenge. It's my very first race. I'll be happy if I can just stay on my feet until the finish.

Ten, nine, eight, seven, six, five, four, three, two, one… Goooooooooo!

That's how ultramarathons start. There's no starter pistol, just a countdown, a big cheer, and we're off.

I fall in behind Pam because, obviously, I have zero experience. I'd never run a race longer than six miles, and that was back when I was a kid. "She knows what she's doing," I tell myself. "So I'm gonna follow her for as long as I can."

But, man, did she take off with those tiny little steps of hers: *tic-tic-tic-tic-tic.* She doesn't take those great big strides that make you say, "Wow, can this lady run!" She keeps the same steady pace practically the whole time. But, as she's already amply demonstrated, once she starts, she pushes through whatever difficulty arises all the way to the finish.

I stay behind her, and it so happens that we do the first marathon together and find ourselves among the top twenty. Shortly afterward, I tell myself, "I feel like I've got some juice in me still. Not that I want to go *too* fast now, but…" So, I open it up a bit and leave Pam behind.

And little by little, I pass one, then five, then ten runners.

At the end of the second marathon, I'd run fifty miles of road, and we get to this big checkpoint that marks the halfway point of the race. My team—my family, that is—is waiting for me there. I stop quickly to take off my running shoes because my feet are in great pain.

My mother nearly faints when she sees them. I don't just have blisters; I have red cherries all over my toes: on top, in between, even under the toenails. It's a bloody mess. "Nothing I can do about it now!" So, I put my shoes back on and continue running.

But, oh boy, do I feel my feet! My socks are soaked in sweat and blisters, and all the rubbing is ripping my skin to shreds. I don't want to think about it. I'm only focused on one thing: getting to the finish.

At around mile sixty, I start having a serious crisis. Having never run a race this long, I've no idea about the sheer amount of wear and tear that comes from doing what I'm trying to do. I'd started training just after Christmas in a cold New York City winter. Here in tropical Florida, at a balmy ninety-five degrees with practically 100 percent humidity, I'm sweating from every pore and I haven't replenished my mineral salts, which shows my utter ignorance. I don't know anything about stuff like that.

"Oh, I'll just eat a power bar here, a banana there, and one way or another, I'll make it through."

Basically, I'd come totally unprepared. Now I'm swelling up and starting to retain water, which is contributing to the huge blisters.

At this point, though, I'm neck and neck with a runner from the Canadian national team, Dave Carver, and since we've been passing each other back and forth, our teams, who are following us in their cars, keep crossing each other. So my mother, who's very worried about me, starts to describe my symptoms to Dave's daughter.

"Don't worry," says the young girl, "just give him a few of these electrolyte tablets, and he'll be alright."

So, I take the tablets, and sure enough, for about an hour, I feel a lot better. I pass Dave, whose daughter had so kindly helped me, and I take off. That's the ultra spirit right there: not cut-throat competitiveness but camaraderie. If you're having a hard time, I'll give you a hand if I can. I'm not going to kick you into the ditch, which is more likely to happen in a lot of other sports.

So, with renewed zest, I keep cruising forward.

I'm nearing the end of the third marathon at about the seventy-five-mile mark when I hear someone yelling, "Go for it, man, c'mon! That Canadian you just passed was in the lead!"

"What?!"

Now *I'm* first. "Alright," I say to myself, "just keep going."

Dave's daughter, however, had only given me two or three electrolyte tablets. When I get to the eighty-mile mark, I'm less than a marathon away, but I'm getting seriously worn out. My armpits are bleeding, my groin is chafed raw, and my ass is as red as a baboon's because I hadn't put any skin-lube on. I'd simply gone out to run. I hadn't prepared for anything else. I just ran.

Between superhuman effort and excruciating pain, I keep moving. But, I get this feeling that something's wrong.

In my utter ignorance I think, "Electrolytes? Sodium. Salt!" So, as soon as I meet my team again, I tell my mother: "Go to the first store you find and get me a package of salt, quick." I rip it open and chug a throat full.

Complete idiocy. From there on, it's a pure massacre. I've been running for fourteen and a half hours. I've covered almost ninety miles on my own two legs. I'm more than halfway into the fourth and last marathon. Only twelve more miles to go. At this pace, that's just a couple of hours, and what's a couple of . . .

Suddenly, I see the road coming at me.

Baaammmmm!

Face plant.

When I wake up, I'm lying in a puddle of vomit with my father slapping me and pulling my tongue out of my throat.

After a while, the ambulance arrives. It's a nasty situation because with hyponatremia, you risk going into a coma and dying. Clearly, it's the end of my race. And while I'm lying there with an IV tube stuck in my arm, I see from the ambulance door in the dead of night, *tic-tic-tic-tic-tic*, Pam Reed's unmistakable stride heading toward the podium.

That was my first ultra, and it was the turning point. Everything that happened after simply followed. Because once you've found your path and you follow it, then you plow ahead, body and soul. I felt I had found what I wanted to do, what I was *meant* to do, and I was going to give it everything I had. Everything, all-in. I loved going ultra, no doubt about it.

Above me hovered the faces of my girlfriend, my sister, and my mother, crying, begging me to stop. "Promise you'll *never* do that again!"

But that, obviously, is how it all started.

This isn't a book about *running*. I'm not interested in *running*, I'm not interested in running a *marathon*—in fact, I've never even run one. But going ultra is something else. It struck me like a bolt of lightning. It inspired me. I want to push myself beyond. I want to understand what lies beyond, and ultra running, as the word itself says, is *beyond* running.

In a time when all the lands have already been explored, all the mountains have been climbed, and every corner of the globe has already been discovered, it seems to me the only real exploration left is the exploration into the depths of your own soul, beyond any physical limit. To find out what we are truly capable of.

2

CHANGING THE COURSE OF THE STREAM

ITALY, 2004–2007

I don't know if we each have a destiny, or if we're all just floating around accidentally—like on a breeze. But I think maybe it's both.

—FORREST GUMP

I was raised in Taggia, a small town on the northwest coast of Italy, where my family owned a floral export business. We didn't sell directly to the guys who wanted a single bouquet. We sold to the people who bought tons of product and then sold it to wholesalers, who then sold it to retailers, who eventually sold it to the public.

I grew up working in my family business, and after completing my studies, that became my full-time job. Sometimes, I worked fifteen-hour days between office sales, the warehouse, and quality-controlling the products. I had to load the trucks, make the sales, buy the goods, and make the price lists. I'd wake up at three in the morning to call Japan before offices closed over there, then I'd stay up until late at night to call the United States. I went on international business trips often, including to New York City and Miami—I worked hard, and I liked it. It was quite an exciting time in my life.

While growing up focusing on the family business, I'd always been shy. Friends made fun of me because I was the last one to get his first kiss. Well, my first kiss became my first girlfriend, and right after my high school graduation, we started dating and moved in together.

Imagine, at twenty years old, I'm living happily with my girl, taking her on vacations to fancy tourist resorts like Santo Domingo, Djerba, and Sharm el-Sheik.

I could buy myself whatever I wanted, and I did. A metallic grey BMW for about fifty grand. Then I got a bike, the Ducati Monster, but I didn't like it, so three months later, I swapped it for the CBR600. Life was good. I worked hard and played hard. I was following the dream.

And so, the years went by. Every summer at the beach, and every weekend partying.

But after a few years, my girlfriend wasn't happy anymore. She decided she needed something else, and she dumped me. I felt really awful for a few months. How can you leave a person just like that? I felt totally bewildered.

Once I came out of the fog from the breakup, it was time for a change.

I was free, but I didn't know exactly what that meant yet.

That's when I got the idea: why not go to Miami and open a new branch of our business?

Sure, I could have stayed home and followed in my parents' footsteps. I could have stayed and had an easy life, a steady career—I would have been just fine. Instead, I felt the urge to do something of my own. I imagined being beside a stream and throwing a rock into it, trying to change its course.

So, I sold my car and my bike and took off for America. In September of 2007, I boarded a plane and left Italy. "I've got to make it with the money I've got. Whatever else I need, I'll earn when I'm there," I told myself. "I'm not going to ask anyone for anything." And if I hadn't found myself looking for an apartment on the other side of the ocean, the next phase of my life in Miami would have looked very different.

* * *

Remember that quote at the end of *Forrest Gump* when the feather flies away? He says, "I don't know if we each have a destiny, or if we're all just floating around accidentally—like on a breeze. But I think maybe it's both." It's so true. Because at any moment, we have the power to renew ourselves. Change, at times, is scary, but we must have the courage to confront it; otherwise, we stay the same. We stop evolving.

As the airplane descended over Miami, I was struck by

the vision of the clean line I could see from the window. On one side were a few miles of beautiful Florida coast, built up, inhabited, well lit, and civilized. On the other side was this huge, dark wilderness—the soul of Florida.

I spent the first two or three weeks in Miami at the house of a friend and client of mine, Willy. He was a little bit older than me, a super fun and easy-going Cuban guy. I slept on the couch in his apartment in Hialeah, which happened to be right near the Everglades, the very swamps I'd seen from above, full of alligators and snakes.

The first thing he did was take me to get a car, and given the small budget I allowed myself, I picked a Cadillac DeVille: '90s, almost vintage, a little beat up. One of those long, white rides that feels like a living room inside. A real pimpmobile. Every day, I'd go back and forth with this car from his house to the industrial area where I worked. I'd always show up looking sharp, suit and tie, to see clients. I was twenty-four, in a new city, going to new places. At that age, it's all great. You put yourself in these situations that are slightly uncomfortable because you know that's exactly how you'll learn to take care of yourself and become independent. It was an exciting time.

After work, I'd head toward the beach in search of an apartment to rent. This is where *the* fateful day comes in. I park my Caddie south of Fifth on Collins Avenue, as I've got some newspaper ads in my pocket and I want to check out a few apartments in the area. I walk north along Ocean Drive, Fifth Street, Sixth, Seventh…typical art deco, low buildings, neon lights, full of tourists. The ocean is on one side with tropical bushes separating the water from Miami's iconic palm-lined sidewalk, complete with girls in super-short shorts on roller-blades and people running or riding bikes.

Booommmmm! Suddenly, there's thunder and lightning, and a storm hits. I look around and see a Johnny Rockets, the hamburger joint, right across the street and jump inside. What a downpour! When it rains there, it's really tropical—a million gallons of water fall in thirty minutes, then the sun pops out again.

So, I order a Coke and wait for it to blow over. I'm minding my own business when…You know how some people just catch your attention? I notice this woman; she must be in her sixties but looking—how would you say?—*fabulous.* I look at her, then look at her again. I've seen her somewhere before…

Then it hits me.

That summer, before leaving home, I watched a reality series called *8th & Ocean* on MTV—which happened to be filmed at the exact spot where I was standing. It was about this businesswoman who had a successful modeling agency and several top models working for her. You followed them as they went to castings; you saw the behind-the-scenes of photo-shoots and the places where they lived. In other words, the whole lifestyle. It was cool.

"Man, I've just arrived and I'm looking at a celebrity!" I didn't give it much more thought than that. Meanwhile, though, she's looking at me, too. Then she gets up and comes to my table.

"Hi, my name's Irene Marie. Won't you come upstairs so we can talk?"

Turns out, she's the owner of the entire building, and right above the street-level hamburger joint, there are two floors of her modeling agency. First, she introduces me to Allie, who sits beside me and examines me for a while.

"Have you ever modeled before?"

"No."

"Ah, that's strange."

Then she goes away and in come two others: an extremely polite former male model, and an Asian woman with balls, if you'll excuse the term. She's very straight forward, all business. We speak for a little while, then Irene comes back with a contract to sign. Exclusive with them. The agency is called Irene Marie Models. How could I say no?

Only a moment before, I'd been sitting downstairs at Johnny Rockets, Coca-Cola in hand, waiting for the downpour to subside, and then, "Come upstairs..."

It was one of those moments of pure excitement when you realize: today, my life changes completely. And it really did. Who says the stream has to keep going the same old route all the way to the end? Sometimes, the stream changes course.

As soon as I got home, I did a little research. Holy shit! This lady represented Marcus Schenkenberg, Tyson Beckford, Joanna Krupa—even Melania Trump. She launched top models worldwide.

And so begins my new career, just like that.

I started working at once. The very next day, I did a shoot for a notorious American magazine with a Russian photographer and four female models. "I am the only guy?! Awesome!"

They fluffed my hair and did me up with a guitar and an unbut-toned psychedelic shirt. Total flower-power style. I looked like Johnny Depp in *Blow*. Ridiculous, but awesome at the same time, like a 1970s rock star.

And that "rock star shoot" became the emblem of how my life would turn out. Because from that point on, I started living like that. My years in Miami can be summarized by three words: sex, drugs, and rock 'n' roll.

3.

THE ACCIDENTAL MODEL

...if you dedicate yourself totally and give things time to mature, you can become whatever you want. That's the most exciting way to live, to grow, to evolve and improve yourself. You let go of what you were, without fear, in order to discover what you're about to become.

I still remember the smell when I walked into the agency, into Irene Marie's big, white room. It smelled of new furniture and fresh paint. The floor had white fur rugs. Photos of ad campaigns and comp cards of every model she represented were taped up on the glass walls. You turned a card around and there you had the name, three or four other photos, and the agency details. Comp cards are like visiting cards that models bring to castings and auditions.

To be honest, I'd never been too interested in fashion. Yeah, once when I was sixteen or seventeen, I'd been approached to go to Milan and give it a try, but my mother said no. She played the good mom, trying to keep me out of that elusive industry.

"That world's not for you," she always said. "One day, you're riding high, the next, they kick your behind!"

So, I never pursued that career path. But it happened anyway.

Fortunately, I didn't open a new branch of the business because shortly afterward, the world economic crisis hit, and revenues crashed 70 to 80 percent. It would have been a bloodbath. Instead, fashion opened up the possibility of creating a fresh path that was entirely my own.

A new life began.

You're still a young kid; you do a shoot here, a shoot there, and you get three, four, five thousand dollars in a snap. For a day's work. What the hell?! I was making good money before, but this was a whole different game. Now I knew eighteen-year-olds who went around with $10,000 in cash in their pocket.

To work as a model, obviously, you have to be a model. For my part, I wasn't a model, so I had to learn how to become one. I guess Irene saw the potential in me, and with her guidance, I slowly transformed myself. And what I learned in the process is that you can transform yourself. You can reinvent yourself as many times as you want. That's the beauty of the American spirit, and it had always attracted me. You can be one thing one day, and the next day, you can decide to do something else. And if you dedicate yourself totally and give things time to mature, you can become whatever you want. That's the most exciting way to live, to grow, to evolve and improve yourself. You let go of what you were, without fear, in order to discover what you're about to become.

At the advice of the booking agency, I had to work on my physique. When I first met Irene, I was much bulkier than a typical fashion model, as I'd been working out at a gym for a few years. I did it to stay in shape, and since my muscles responded particularly well, I got to the point where my trainer asked if I was interested in competing as a bodybuilder.

When it came down to it, though, I said, "No, thanks." Because usually, you don't do bodybuilding in a natural way—you do it by juicing yourself up. And I always thought, "What's the point of that?"

So, when this modeling career presented itself, I continued working on my body, sculpting it in a different way. I found it fascinating. It's an art, really. The art of shaping the proportions of your own body to create a sense of harmony. You try to build up a little extra volume here, get more toned in the arms, add a little mass on the front of the shoulders, tighten up the back, cut the abs, work on the hamstrings…

"Today, full cardio, and I won't lift because I have to lose some weight."

"Tomorrow, I've got a shoot, so I'll take a laxative this evening to be totally shredded in the morning."

I learned that even when you're in shape, your stomach will always be a little swollen, even if you eat a little. So, the night before a shoot, you've got to fast in order to be totally ripped and get abs that look like they've been Photoshopped.

Through learning quickly and training hard, I started getting a lot of work. In the beginning, I just worked in Miami, mostly for fashion catalogues. Clients arrived from Europe during the winter months, when it was cold over there. They came down to Florida to photograph catalogues for the next spring and summer collections. And there we were—all tan and in tip-top shape.

I did a few ad campaigns, mainly stuff in bathing suits, and editorials for big magazines where you're at the beach or poolside. I was always bare-chested or with an open shirt. I was one of those "guys with the eight pack."

Once I started working my way up to high fashion, though, the booking agency told me I needed to lean down some more to fit into a tight blazer and these skinny trousers. I had already started slimming down, shaping my body differently, and to fit into these clothes, I had to shed about twenty more pounds—all of which was muscle. This takes determination because getting a body with such a low percentage of fat and those kinds of shapes isn't easy. When I began, I was bulky, but in the course of six months to a year, my structure changed completely and became more "harmonious."

Buff is beefy. If you think of Michelangelo's famous sculpture of David, he is totally harmonious. You can see that he's cut: the arms, the chest, the abs, the legs, the calves. He's almost like an athlete. Michelangelo based him on the ideal Greek hero. And the modern fashion industry still looks for the same forms, like the heroes of ancient mythology: Adonis, Perseus, or Hercules.

For me, when I embarked on that career, the ideal reference point was Marcus Schenkenberg, one of the most famous male supermodels of all time.

Not sure if it's the way I was raised or simply how I am, but when I do something, I have to give it all I've got. I'd chosen that path, so I put my head down and went for it completely. What's the point of doing things halfway? It'd just be a waste of time.

So, that was my approach from the very beginning: total dedication. Because even in fashion, there's no free ride. Many people think, "Oh, if you've got a pretty face, it's easy to be a model." Not at all. Nothing is easy. Being successful in fashion means a lot of hard work. It's a world I had to learn to navigate—I learned how to behave, how to present myself. If you want to be widely successful, obviously, you need a dose of good luck and good looks, but most of all, you have to be professional. So, I learned the art. I was always on the ball, always on time to castings, on time for work, and I maintained good relations with the agencies and bookers who got me the work. I learned better and better how to take care of my body.

The more professional you are and the more effort you put in, the more successful you'll be. And personal relationships are very important at that level—in work and in life. You've got to be easy going, open, relatable. I'd actually learned this from my parents during the years I worked in the family business. In fact, I now recognize they were my biggest teachers.

Aside from the physique and professionalism, what does it really mean to be a good model? You also have to be an actor. You have to learn how to move and how to look casual in front of a camera. You have to follow the photographer's instructions and give the clients what they want. That's where the skill comes in. I learned this quickly as well, and things really started to click.

That's when it really began, a period that was like...
Wooooooooooowwww!!!!!

You can imagine. There I was, minding my own business when this perfect wave comes in. And I catch it and start riding it—big time!

4.

BIG BEAR

I wish I had known this feeling of 'comfort makes you weak' before I started riding that wave of luxury and excess.

When I train, I enjoy myself. I get to go outdoors and be on my own. Sure, it's tough doing these three-, five-, six-, and eight-hour training sessions, but if you're not also enjoying them, then they pretty much become impossible, don't they?

As far as the inner quest is concerned, it's important to retreat a little from society. When we're on display in front of everyone, this can be pretty hard, whereas if you concentrate only on yourself, you begin to listen to and understand yourself. Going ultra is a means that allows you to discover yourself in the rawest conditions, under fatigue, effort, and pain.

And then those magical moments happen. You'll never

remember what you did that random Thursday night you went to the pub downtown to drink a beer, but you'll never forget when you popped out of that trail and a glacier opened up in front of you with a herd of bighorn sheep coming down. Or that river that was a color you didn't even know existed—what shade of turquoise is this?!—the color of sparkling ice water cascading from the mountains.

Or…that morning you found yourself face to face with a bear.

Now, in my training forays, I've encountered a great deal of wildlife: deer, eagles, coyotes, rattlesnakes. The mountain lion, for instance, is a real son of a bitch!

However, I had one of the most beautiful experiences in the mountains of Southern California in a place called Big Bear. That's one of my favorite training grounds. I head up there with my one-man tent, in which you lie down like you're in a coffin. Some people travel around doing the van life, which is probably a lot more comfortable, but I like the simplicity of my little, blue tent. Before all my races, I try to do one or two weeks like that, in retreat, just focusing on training and doing my thing.

They say Genghis Khan didn't even deign to enter the cities he conquered. When the deed was done, he sent his men ahead while he remained outside. He slept out in the open in a ger, the traditional tent of the nomadic Mongols. This was because his strength came from "the eternal blue sky."

For me, Nature is an absolute necessity. When you're out there, you can finally detach from any social construct. The mind is free, so you can truly get in touch with yourself. You focus on what you really want to do. There are no distractions—no voices blaring from the radio, the TV, or the telephone. Just the gurgling of water, the wind rustling through the woods. You watch the grass sway, the spiraling climb of a pair of butterflies. They may seem like trivial, little things, but if you stay there and learn to appreciate them, those things give you peace. And strength.

I like living at my own pace, taking my time, getting in touch with my body, listening carefully to its needs. If I'm hungry and it's time to eat, I eat; if I'm hungry and it's not time to eat, I control myself.

I get ready.

Training in the mountains is beautiful; it's not like running down city streets. And what's more, you're at altitude, which is important. The little town of Big Bear is more than 6,750 feet above sea level, and from there you can take trails that head up to nearly ten thousand feet. It's not just beauty that surrounds you, but the air is different, more rarefied. There's less oxygen up there, which makes you develop more red blood cells. So, when you go back down for your race, your blood is capable of transporting more oxygen, and if the body is more oxygenated, it's much more resilient. Oxygen is our fuel. This is one of the secrets of high-altitude training.

That's why Kenyans have always been great long-distance runners because they train at more than nine thousand feet in Iten in the Rift Valley. That's their Mecca. When they descend to a city like Berlin to run a marathon, they practically feel the oxygen particles hit them in the face!

In Big Bear, I wake up really early and go for a run, then maybe around mid-morning, I head to Starbucks in the nearby town centre because they've got Wi-Fi there. I can catch up with my email and do some work. In the evening, I train again and do yoga or sit outside at my table—which is a big rock. As soon as it gets dark, I start the fire, heat up my dinner, gaze at the stars a bit, then go to bed. Two weeks straight, just like this. Alone with nothing else but me, my tent, and the fire. I'm outside all day. It's a wonderful feeling.

Sure, a bed with a mattress would be more comfortable, but your body becomes stronger by sleeping on the hard ground. When you stretch out on the Earth, you feel energized, while comfort makes you weak.

One morning, I'm flying downhill when just around a tight switchback, I see this huge butt right in front of me. Enormous. It's a black bear as big as a car! I screech to a halt, kicking up a cloud of dust, and fortunately, the beast gets scared and starts running away. After about twenty yards, though, he turns around to look at me. "What the hell am *I* running away for?!" he seems to be saying.

So I stand there, totally petrified.

Fortunately, there's a tree nearby, so I creep behind it to hide. If he attacks, there's nothing I can do. If he wants to find me, he'll sniff me out. But I don't run away—I stay there and wait.

After a while, I begin to clap my hands. "C'mon, buddy,

would you move out of the way, please? I got nothing against you. This isn't a challenge or anything, I just have to get by. You go your way; I'll go mine."

And just like that, the big bear kindly went away.

5.

LIVING IN LA-LA-LAND

MIAMI, 2008

I called it "La-la-land" because there you are, living what you'd always imagined to be "the good life," completely careless. It was the stereotype of "the dream."

Let's go back to the first few weeks in Miami for a moment because throughout this new accidental career, a whirlwind romance was developing.

I'd barely been in Miami for two weeks. I'd signed with the agency, and then the following weekend, I met her in a club. A stunning woman, a former WWE wrestler, strong and bursting at the seams, who rolled with the socialites.

So, we started hanging out and dated for a few months until a problem arose: my visa was about to expire. "Don't worry, baby!" she said. "Why don't we go ahead and get married now? That way you can stay." After all, we had already moved in together. And just like that, in the blink of an eye, I got my green card, and my life in America was official.

I found a great apartment for us a block from the beach on the fourteenth floor of a skyscraper with a pool. Ocean view? Even better! We lived on Sixty-Nineth Street in a section of Miami Beach where the island is thinnest. The balcony of the building faced south, so we could see the ocean and beach on the left, the bay with its islands to the right, South Beach right in front of us, and Downtown in the distance. In other words, it was an incredible place.

We started living it up, having fun, and going out with models and celebrities. I have to admit, when you're young, that kind of lifestyle feels spectacular because you're going from a beach party to a pool party to another club party. Total freedom without a care in the world.

We went to agency parties where they rented out entire clubs, and models and agents all hung out together. One of the best ones I remember was on Halloween when I went dressed as a gladiator, wearing only a shield, a pair of sandals, and a little skirt. There were women going around practically nude with only a splash of paint on them, thong panties, and stickers on their nipples. That was the type of world we rolled in. I called it "La-la-land" because there you are, living what you'd always imagined to be *the good life*," completely careless. It was the stereotype of "*the dream.*"

The PR people of the clubs invite you to come there all the time to boost their image, so you get to swing about town and everything is free—everything is up for grabs, everything is given. Bottles of champagne, Patron and Grey Goose, tables at restaurants, because you're a model and your presence makes them look cool. We'd go for dinner, rack up a bill for thousands, pay nothing, and then just get up. "Thanks for dinner, buddy—see you next week!"

Of course, we all played the game, as it was a good deal for them, too. It's what the PR companies do, and we lived off of it. This PR guy calls you, another one wants you, you go to a party here, a dinner there. Sometimes, there were pool parties at the Delano or the Shore Club or The W—all the "in" places. They were the "high-class" hotels, so to speak, and held private parties at their pools on weekends. And there you'd find hip DJs; big, buff, iron-pumping guys; and touched-up girls with fake breasts. Everyone in bathing suits and bikinis already soaked in vodka at two o'clock in the afternoon.

Well, that's how we spent our days. We were invited everywhere along with these other guys I used to hang out with: Edd from Eastern Europe, Jon the Canadian, and Marco from Costa Rica. Happy hours, fancy dinners, and clubbing at night. There were lines a mile long outside, but we'd just walk straight up to the bouncer at the door. "Hey, man, how's it going?" And he'd unhook the red velvet cord to let us right in. We were on top of the world.

Everywhere we went, the doors swung wide open.

6.

MODEL SEASON

It was a perfect moment, and it looked like happiness.

At first, I was still tied to my old values, so I was always the one to say, "No, no, no…" But then, the whole thing finally overwhelmed me. That lifestyle makes you lose touch with reality. You're floating in a bubble on an idyllic tropical island where it's always summer, and you're in shorts and a T-shirt—or without even that—every single day.

Waking up late (because you partied until dawn), you start to get ready. If there's a shoot, you do the shoot; otherwise, you drop in at the agency to say hi or go to a few castings. I was constantly on the move, usually cruising down on my longboard.

About a year had passed since I arrived in Miami, and I

was chosen, along with two female models, to do a miniseries, a reality show called *Model Season*. You can still find some episodes of it on YouTube. So, when I was walking around the streets or going to castings, people would stop me.

"Hey, Mickey!"

We were *almost famous*—for what it was worth—at a local level. Miami's South Beach is basically like a village, so everyone ends up knowing everyone else. And for me, work was going well, and I was beginning to build a decent reputation.

"Can you believe it, I'm here!" I'd sometimes think to myself. "I came from a sleepy, little town in Italy, and now, I'm here. I made it!"

I could work for two days and be set for months. Sometimes, I almost felt bad about it. "My friends back home work a year to get what I earn in a day." It definitely made me think, "Well, lucky me, I guess."

It was a perfect moment, and it looked like *happiness*.

Then, in 2009, my career really took off. I'd go back and forth between Miami, Milan, and New York. Good money started coming in, so I moved from Sixty-Nineth Street to the very heart of South Beach. And I got a new car. I sold that beat up Cadillac DeVille and got myself a nice golden Mercedes.

In the meantime, our circle of friends kept expanding. This person knows that person who knows another person who's even more famous and even richer and even "bigger." So, they'd take you for a ride on their yacht, and they'd want you in their entourage. And one day, you find yourself backstage at David Guetta's concert dancing on the table next to P. Diddy.

But the craziest parties of all were in the private mansions of the super-rich. You'd see things there that made your head spin.

And the party that would really open the floodgates for me was about to begin.

7.

THE QUEEN'S PARTY

But then you find yourself in this situation, and what do you do?

Through a friend of a friend of a friend, on New Year's Eve, I met this Russian lady. She was in her mid-forties maybe, all touched up and still very attractive. At the time, my relationship status was somewhat "ambiguous," and she too was married—for what it's worth in those circles. Her husband would go off with his little model friends, while she had her own stable of studs.

Every once in a while, when a new male model came to town, she'd show him around and take him out shopping. She was a bit of a sugar mama, let's say. Then, in her limo, she'd have him chauffeured back to her wonderful mansion and have her way with him. Our friendship began pretty much like this, except that I quickly explained my situation to her, saying I didn't want to put my relationship in jeopardy at that moment. She seemed to appreciate my "No," and we immediately became friends.

Indeed, we became good friends. We'd even go for a quiet lunch on Lincoln Road just to talk and be together without ever "getting together."

She was beautiful, sure, but more than that, she was one of those people who had great *savoir faire*. In fact, she and I always had a relationship of mutual admiration because in any case, she did what she liked and she was very good at playing her game. So, kudos to her.

She had started from nothing, charged valiantly toward the United States, thrown herself into social life, got married to a rich guy, and *poof,* she'd become a millionaire.

"The Queen" together with her King had exorbitant wealth at their disposal, and every once in a while, they threw otherworldly parties. Real shows, spectacles that cost hundreds of thousands of dollars.

But the one to which we were invited to that night was a private party. An exclusive party to celebrate the Queen's birthday.

Her palace was on one of the three elite, artificially created islands in the Bay of Miami: Palm Island, Star Island, and Hibiscus Island. Just south of those islands are the Keys islands, where one day I would run my very first ultra. But right now, nothing was further from my mind. Al Capone had lived there, and now Sylvester Stallone, Shaquille O'Neal, Martha Stewart,

P. Diddy, and a host of the richest people all owned houses there—the ones you might call the American elite. They had mega estates worth twenty, thirty, and forty million dollars with yachts parked in front of them that were so huge you could barely see their houses.

A bridge takes you to the entrance of the island, where there's a big gate with security. You have to show ID and say where you're going and why. To avoid all that trouble, the Queen sent her Rolls Royce to pick us up at home, complete with a sharp-looking chauffeur wearing his cap in good ol' fashion. He opened the door for us, we got into the car and enjoyed a glass of champagne on the ride. When we got to the island, we slipped right through the gate, no questions asked. There were already Lamborghinis, Phantoms, and convertible Bentleys parked in front of the mansion. A thought flashed through my mind, "If we'd pulled up in my gold Mercedes, we would have looked like paupers!"

That night, there were only fifteen of us. There were more servants than guests: a butler, the chef in the kitchen, the waiters with their heads bowed in deference. As soon as we got there, they offered us trays full of hors d'oeuvres. There were high counters of marble with appetizers and rivers of champagne on them. Veuve Clicquot flowed like water. I felt a bit uneasy, but whatever, the evening got underway.

We were seated at the dining table in that endless living room with a view of Miami Bay. As the servants brought in the different courses, the chef would emerge to give a whole long, elaborate explanation about what we were about to eat…*a chunk of meat and a few leaves of salad*! But he made it sound amazing.

We ate with all the waiters hovering around ready to take our plates away as soon as we were done. Then the Queen, the person we were celebrating, stood up.

"And now," she declared, "it's time for dessert!"

She disappeared only to return moments later with a big, silver tray she placed right in the middle of the table. I was busy talking to people and didn't really notice anything at first, also because there was still catering all around. It was as if the guests couldn't have cared less.

"But…!?" I squinted my eyes as I looked at everyone for a second, perplexed.

The "dessert" looked like the Mont Blanc, only it wasn't snow I was looking at. You know this stuff exists, of course, because you catch glimpses of it going around when you go to parties. But this was different. This was *à la Scarface* when Tony Montana has a mountain of coke on a platter in front of him and he plunges his face into it. That's pretty much exactly how this was.

So now imagine, our little group of guests sitting there—a few laughs, and the game begins.

I'd never done it before. I'd managed to resist for a long time. But then you find yourself in this situation, and *what do you do*? Everyone's high, openly flying at that point. There's loud music, you're having fun, you chat with one person, chat with another, drink another glass of champagne…until you end up trying a line, too.

"Let's see what this is all about," you tell yourself. After all, it's something new. Go ahead; try it. Just a little bit. It's not like you're doing anything bad. Bing! And you start sliding down the slippery slope. You do a line, then another, then three, four, five. Until it seems perfectly normal, like eating biscuits by the fireside. That's how it happened—one thing just led smoothly to another.

That first year had been a blast, but I still tried to remain true to the values I'd been raised with. Yeah, sure, we went out and drank and partied, but it was always fairly under control up until that moment. The others did their thing, but not me. I didn't smoke. I didn't do anything, really. I resisted because throughout my childhood, my group of friends and I were raised by parents who went out of their way to protect family values and keep a healthy lifestyle. I'd left home at nineteen, but I lived a mile down the road from my parents. Even when I worked, I'd always go back home to my mother's for lunch. Then I moved to Miami and stepped into this razzle-dazzle world.

And here I was.

This birthday party marked my entry into the wild. I let go of the reins and took off. And for almost a year, I lived a thousand miles an hour.

Meanwhile, there were fifteen guests in the Queen's castle, and what happened next…well, it was crazy. It was the stuff that you only see in movies.

8.

A THOUSAND MILES AN HOUR

MIAMI, 2008–2009

Life moves pretty fast. If you don't stop and look around once in a while, you could miss it.

—FERRIS BUELLER

I flew off the handle and spent the next few months in a haze. Wherever I went, it was hard-party time. We'd start with a dinner, maybe, then head to a club and keep going all night. When it closed, we'd move on to an after-hours party. Sometimes, we partied for two or three days straight. From one person's house to another's pool to yet another dinner, a club here, a breakfast there. Those were fast times. Meeting loads of people, famous producers, musicians, partying with celebrities …

Sometimes fifteen or twenty of us would go party together, and the whole club would just stop and stare, as we truly partied like rock stars. We were young, wild, and free. We'd climb up on the tables and dance like there was no tomorrow, music blasting, flirting, drinking, going to the bathroom for a toot—or not even bothering with the bathroom, actually. Everything was right out there in the open, no holding back, like we didn't give a fuck about anything. Nothing at all.

Outside, the world was going through some hard times. You heard people talk about recession and companies going bankrupt. But we remained lucky in those years and were able to live it up because the fashion and entertainment industries kept going strong.

Then, there were the socialites. The people who ran in certain social circles were pretty much always the same. When you enter the fashion scene, people begin to recognize you here and there, and you live off the notoriety. Because apart from the fashion connection, there's the fact that you know so-and-so. All that trouble just to attract attention and impress others!

It's really quite a shallow world at that level. It's all about appearances—having the most expensive car, the most beautiful people around, and going to fancy parties so it looks like they have the perfect life.

They might have twenty people in tow. They take you to a high-end restaurant and, for starters, order two bottles of vodka and four bottles of champagne as if they're mineral water, while those bottles might run about a thousand dollars each. It's insane! In those places, the food is enormously overpriced just because the chef is famous, and you end up hardly eating anything as the portions are so meager. When you walk out of the place, you have to go for a sandwich on the corner because you're still starving…Some things I just didn't understand.

The Queen was often around, as we were friends and she was the main sponsor.

So, that was the life of revelry that I was presented with, and not just every once in a while but five or six nights a week. Monday was the day of rest because Tuesday was a big party night at Mokai, which was *the* club in South Beach at the time.

We had a riot in those years—twenty-five, twenty-six years old and living large.

Not all models had it like we did, though. But I was lucky enough to become friends with club owners and celebs, so we managed to live particularly high on the food chain. Right at the top, actually. We were going full speed, rock 'n' roll! And everywhere we went, people knew who we were.

In that scene, coke is like the daily bread. Alcohol and coke get rid of inhibitions, which explains why there's so much madness in South Beach. And lots of flirting and out-of-control promiscuity. Couples don't even get upset about it—I'll shut one eye, you shut the other. Relationships are freakishly frivolous.

Among top models, and not just top ones, blow is a great help. First, it keeps you wide awake; second, it keeps you from eating, as it kills your appetite. It "chisels your fat away." That's why you see a lot of models and TV personalities who are as thin as rails—it's not always because of exercise and diet. It's not unusual to see signs at fashion shows that read: *PLEASE DON'T FEED THE MODELS!*

Coke is the norm. Then it somehow becomes part of the lifestyle, and if you don't do it, then you're cut out. You can't go to parties where everyone is totally high and be the only sober one, watching.

The girls, especially, eat so little they're practically surviving on vodka and coke. No beer and no wine because those make you swell. But you're playing on the edge there. In fact, you can only sustain that kind of lifestyle for a short while. For women, it was so unhealthy they'd often stop having their periods.

They're portraying that *beauty* stereotype, but they're unable to have kids. It's a natural safety measure. If you're too skinny, your body says, "No fat...no kids; otherwise either you or the child will die. You just don't have enough sustenance to bear life." It's pure insanity, but it's perfectly normal in those circles.

I went through some real hardcore situations. But it felt normal—it was so accepted, it was almost routine. I lived a period of complete *sbagascio*—a fitting word from the Ligurian dialect, which means "just letting go completely."

And so, life veered into a frenetic downward spiral. The crazy thing is that not far away—not on the other side of the world, but just a couple of blocks over—there were people who had nothing. Because there's a lot of poverty in Miami, too. There's the ghetto and desolation and no-go zones. Can you imagine? Living in poverty while others have so much money they don't know what the hell to do with it.

That kind of lifestyle completely cuts you off from reality.

It took me a while to figure it out. But, I eventually got there.

9.

RICH KID CRYING IN THE BATHROOM

WINTER, 2009

If everything is always easy, you appreciate nothing at all.

During that period, a couple of episodes happened that felt like two slaps followed by a punch in the face.

The first slap came pretty much one year after the Queen's birthday when she invited us to yet another party. This time, it was not just for a select few but for two or three hundred people.

On this occasion, there was a circus theme, so there were jugglers on one side, a fire eater on the other, and trapeze artists flying above. They'd even brought in a couple of white tigers in chains.

It was out of this world. But that's how they kept themselves busy.

The mansion was enormous, so there was room for everybody. They'd opened the garden with a pool that looked out onto the bay where their four-story yacht was docked. There was catering and rivers of champagne, as usual. Dancers and strippers were placed all around, doing nothing, just there, looking, well…slutty. And the girls from the catering were dressed like bunnies. And two gigantic bodybuilders in ridiculous skin-tight suits greeted you at the gate. Stuff like that. Nonsense. Pure nonsense.

The "who's who" began with loads of people rolling in, and the car park filling up quickly. On the opposite side, to the left, there was a beautiful wall of water that fell into a little pond full of goldfish, like in a Japanese garden. You went down a catwalk right through the middle, like you were walking on water. Then, you entered through a large door into an immense living room with a glass window looking over the shimmering bay ahead.

Music played at full blast, reverberating from speakers inside and out, and we started partying. Then, we came across one of the Queen's closest friends, a young man with whom she hung out often. With his blond curls, he looked like a little angel, always well-groomed, refined, with elegant clothes and smooth skin that had never seen a day of work. He was too busy spending his days getting facials at the spa. He was another one of those people who always got everything he wanted at his immediate demand and to his satisfaction.

The evening carried on, and eventually, whoever was tired

went home, and whoever was too high or drunk spent the night there at the mansion, where there were more rooms than anybody even knew. I stayed over of course, and we lay down in crowded beds.

In the morning, I wake up, and it seems that everyone's gone, but then I hear some odd noises, so I go to the bathroom to see what's going on. And there he is, the blond angel, sitting alone on the floor with his back against the wall, drenched in vomit, crying. He's having a hysterical fit.

"What's the matter?"

"It's nothing, nothing…" he keeps repeating as he continues to cry.

But it's quite clear that he's not well at all, poor guy. *Poor* in a manner of speaking because he's got more money than you can even imagine. But he wakes up every morning realizing he still hasn't found the thing that truly makes him content in life. Because clearly, in spite of the millions he spends on shopping, the private jet, the fancy cars, and the women or the men that he can buy, he still hasn't found what really matters.

"So, what's the point?" I ask myself. "What's the point of it all?!"

I met a lot of people like him in those years who literally did nothing in life, absolutely nothing. Nothing at all. They didn't even have to work because they had so much money, and they could have as much free time as they wished. So, they did whatever they wanted but then couldn't find a point to life. In the end, they woke up each morning to answer these questions: "Who am I? What am I doing with this life of mine?"

He was totally depressed, an alcoholic, always zonked on Xanax and who knows what other pills because he just couldn't stand himself.

That image touched me deeply.

There he was, alone, with no objective. No goals or ambitions. If you've already got everything, it's easy to lose your desire to live altogether. You lose all meaning. You might have everything you want, but if your life has no meaning, you'll never feel fulfilled. Or purposeful.

That's what the blond angel made me understand—that poor guy.

10.

DANCING ON TABLES

SPRING, 2009

They say if you don't lose yourself, you can't find yourself.

The second slap in the face came totally unexpectedly. It came during yet another night at a club while dancing on tables—again—with a bottle of Grey Goose in hand and lots of hot models swirling around.

"Yeah, dude, you're totally one of us!" yells one of the guys there, putting his arms around my shoulders.

Ding-ding-ding-ding-ding...

In that very instant, my alarm bell went off. Hell no, I'm not! I don't want to be like that. I'm sorry. Because I look at you, already getting on in years, and you're still standing on tables, snorting coke until dawn. But hopefully, I won't be. Nothing against you if that's what rocks your world, but I don't want to be doing this twenty years from now.

That guy's comment pulled me back into myself. Time slowed down as I came to that realization. It was a real turning point. I'd had a lot of fun, it had been a great experience, but right then and there, a moment of epiphany came, and I understood there was more to life than this.

If all you ever do is party, after a while, the party's no longer a party.

"What the hell are we always celebrating?" you ask yourself.

Parties are fun when they happen every now and then to celebrate something. But if life's a constant party, it becomes monotonous. Even the pleasure of celebrating fades away.

Those people with whom I went out and had fun, with whom I didn't think much about anything, had total freedom to take whatever they liked, went wherever they pleased, and said and did whatever they wanted. Everything was given to them, and they were entitled to it all. But it transformed them. The more they had, the bigger they felt and the less respect they had for others—and for themselves, too. You end up doing so much that you lose your values. And when you lose your values, you lose your virtues, and you lose contact with your true self.

That's what I felt, and that's why that very night I decided I needed to leave Miami.

All those episodes led me to reevaluate my basic needs. After so many parties, so many things, so much insanity, nonsense, and experiences—or whatever you want to call them—honestly, I wouldn't change a single thing about that chapter of my life, not a second. Each and every one of those experiences helped me to grow and to mature.

For a while, in fact, it had been exhilarating. I dove in headfirst. If you don't try to do something all the way, you'll never really know what it's about, so I plunged in. It was a life right out of fiction or TV, those things you only see in gossip columns...Isn't that what's sold as the image of success, of what we're supposed to be?

Once you get there, though, you soon realize the life of sex, drugs, and rock 'n' roll isn't all it's cut out to be. It comes at a price, then comes the big let down. I'm guessing that's why Jim Morrison died and Kurt Cobain shot himself in the head and why lots of other stars ended up committing suicide. The depression that plagues so many rich and famous people is due to the fact that when they manage to achieve what they've been told is the greatest thing in the world, they suddenly realize it's not the answer.

It's all just an image. If you cannot find a deeper purpose, it's just a façade. But what's behind it? If that's all you've got, it's not happiness. When you're living inside it, you realize the walls are made of cardboard, and there aren't even any rooms. And the bigger the façade, the more you hear the emptiness echoing.

At least that's the effect it had on me.

The instant that guy pulled me to him and said, "yeah, dude, you're totally one of us!" I landed hard with my feet on the ground.

Baaaammm! I was wide awake.

No more for me, thank you. I'm out.

11.

THE SWEET SMELL OF THE CITY

APRIL, 2009

I'd left a world that started to drag me down for something fresh and stimulating and exciting.

Despite the underlying personal crisis I was facing, my career was really taking off. I worked a lot in Miami and was earning good money. But I needed to get away from that scene. I didn't like what I was doing, and I despised who I was becoming. That whole wild adventure in Miami lasted about a year.

During this period, I started going back and forth to New York almost every week. That spring, I must have taken over twenty flights. I was constantly on a plane. Practically twice a week, I took a plane to NYC, then a cab straight to a shoot for the day. As soon as it was over, I hopped in another cab for the airport to catch a flight back to South Beach in order to make it back for another shoot the next day. Constantly on a plane, back and forth.

Aside from the chaos of what daily life in Miami had become, I'd also reached the point where the work in Miami wasn't enough to take my career to the next level. It was a seasonal market where it's easy to start working, and you're not competing with the "big fish." But if you want to work at the top level, you have to get on the London, Paris, Milan, Tokyo, and New York circuits.

On top of that, Irene Marie Models went bankrupt and closed during the recession in the spring of 2009. Fortunately, there was no shortage of offers for me. The very next day, there were other agencies ready to sign me up. I chose Next, which, together with Wilhelmina and Ford Models, was probably one of the biggest agencies in the world.

So, that spring, a few months before my twenty-sixth birthday, I moved to New York City. And work went very well there. I was at the top of my career. I'd left a world that had started to drag me down, and I was looking for something new.

And I was in really good shape. *A-ma-zing* shape. If you think of a body in artistic terms, I had reached the apex of symmetry and harmony. And I knew it. That, in fact, was why after only a week of being in New York, I ended up doing a shoot with Steven Klein, one of the most famous fashion photographers in the world who was also one of Madonna's best friends.

There were other guys who came in from Milan and Paris and were more famous or sought after than I was at the moment, but they ended up putting me there with Marlon Teixeira, a Brazilian supermodel who was *the* top male model at the time, and Ginnifer Goodwin, a Hollywood actress. We did a shoot, the three of us, two guys and a girl. "This is unbelievable!" There I was in the Big Apple working with the biggest agencies and best photographers in the world.

I'd prepared myself for the job; I'd worked hard for it. That's why I keep saying it's all a matter of total dedication and preparation. When the other guy's asleep, you wake up. When the other guy wakes up, you train. When the other guy is training, you train more.

* * *

It was a cold spring day in 2009 when I arrived in New York. This time, I planned to make it my home. I only had one small suitcase with me. The rest of my stuff was still in the apartment in Miami. I wore my tight-fitting gray trench coat, shiny leather shoes, skinny black trousers (to show off my body), a nice sweater, and a shoulder bag over the coat. I was stylish. I walked around looking like I was meant to be there.

I landed in La Guardia, then I took the subway to Midtown. I got out at Thirty-Fourth Street because the agency was on Twenty-Seventh and Park Avenue. I didn't know the city very well and walked with a map in my hand. I saw Penn

Station, and then from there, I walked a couple of avenues over, a few blocks down, and there it was.

I was inebriated by the smell of New York when I first arrived—a sweet smell. It wasn't the stench of a city; it was more like a fragrance. I loved it. It was something fresh and stimulating and exciting.

I arrived at the agency early in the morning. I'd taken the five o'clock flight from Miami with my friend Edd, the Eastern European guy. We'd left together for New York that very morning. He was still without an agency, but I had this hookup with Jason Kanner, one of the top agents in New York at the time. For male models, Kanner was considered *the* booker. If you look up the top male models in the world, they're mostly under his wing.

So anyway, I walk into his office, and we talk for a while, and he seems pretty pleased.

"OK, let's do this!" he says energetically. He sends me to a shoot right away, that very morning. Once the shoot with that photographer is over, I'm in a coffee shop getting something to eat, and the booker calls me again. He tells me I've got another appointment on such-and-such street at two o'clock.

"Alright!"

I pick up my stuff and go. Two hours later, he's calling me again, "Look, as soon as you're finished, you have to go to this other place."

"Oh, OK, sure!"

I'd been up and running since four in the morning, and this guy had me do three shoots and two castings on the same day. To add to the stress, one appointment was downtown and the other was uptown. I had to catch the subway, change trains, walk two blocks, climb four flights of stairs, do the shoot, go back down, come back out—all in those shiny leather shoes. I finished around 7:30 that evening, and we didn't even think about where we were going to stay that night. Well, really, we hadn't thought about where we'd stay for the next few weeks while we searched for a place to live! "We'll find some friends," we'd figured. I call my buddy Edd, and he's all excited. "Our buddy Jay invited us to stay at his place!"

"OK, excellent. Where are you?"

"One Hundred and Forty-Seventh Street."

I was down by Union Square. Ugh! So, I took the subway uptown, changed at Times Square, then took the One train, which makes every friggin' stop on the West Side. *Every single one of them*!

As I walk out of the subway, I look down on the ground, and there's a little piece of folded paper. Without thinking too much of it, I pick it up. It's a hundred-dollar bill.

"Wow, this must be a sign!" I tell myself.

There were a bunch of drug dealers outside the subway exit, and one of them must have inadvertently dropped it. It was a bit of a sketchy neighborhood, but after a short walk, I finally get there, exhausted, and I crash on Jay's couch. He was a very welcoming, super-shredded black dude who also worked as a model in the city. We ended up staying with him in Harlem for a couple of weeks while I worked and looked for an apartment.

In New York, I worked hard. All day, every day. I left at

seven or eight in the morning and got back at seven or eight in the evening. I was always on the move. And all that time I was in New York, I never partied. I went to one single party, and that was enough for me. I'll get to that story in a moment.

12.

LEARNING FROM THE BEST

MAY, 2009

Don't count the days; make the days count.

—Muhammad Ali

I found an apartment near Battery Park, a few blocks away from Wall Street, with a spectacular view of the Statue of Liberty. It was a beautiful building with a doorman, a warm lobby, reception, and an enormous gym with a sauna. And since things were going well, I kept my place in Miami, too.

My wife decided to move to New York as well despite the serious crisis we'd fallen into. We decided to go on a trip to St. Barts together to see if we could straighten things out a bit, but with its posh vibe and exclusive feel, Saint Barts wasn't the ideal place for reestablishing a connection. Our relationship didn't make sense anymore.

To get away from all of that, I often hung out with my friend Edd and another friend JC, a Brazilian top model. The two of them had done major ad campaigns for Givenchy, Diesel, D2, and the like. I learned a lot from those guys, as they had a very driven mindset. They were highly competitive, so I paid close attention to their physical preparation. I improved even more just by spending time with them. In fact, they were both among the most sought-after models.

Brazilian male models in general were in the highest demand, like Eastern European women. Russian girls, for instance, have a look that really lends itself to modeling, with very delicate features you can transform in a second with a good make-up artist. You can really play with their looks.

With guys, in the end, it's more a question of physical preparation. And so, that's what we did. In fact, very often, the three of us spent the whole day together, working out. We developed our own rigorous training routine, and our lifestyles were no longer linked to social life, drinking, drugs, and partying till dawn. We got back to a high level of balance and professionalism.

It was during this period with them that I started to rediscover my passion for running. Every morning, we'd wake up early, meet at my place at seven, and go jogging up the West Side along the Hudson River. Other times, we'd go around the bottom of Manhattan and run on the East Side, where we'd cross the Brooklyn Bridge, run up to the Manhattan Bridge, and cross back into the city through Chinatown. We'd maybe do a little shopping for fresh produce there before heading up Broadway and then back home.

So, I slowly got into running. Not big time, just maybe three or four miles at a time. They were basically fun, warm-up runs because sometimes we wanted to get outside, and we didn't want to do all of our running on treadmills at the gym.

I'd meet these guys in the morning, then sometimes in the afternoon, we'd get together again over at my apartment building, which had a rooftop where we could lounge and catch some sun because of course, we always needed to be tan. We'd bring jump ropes along, too, then head back to the gym for another round of push-ups and pull-ups. Afterward, we would go into the sauna to come out looking more chiseled than ever. We'd often even have dinner together.

Our day basically consisted of castings, shootings, and training sessions.

And the next day, we'd do it all over again.

13.

THE SPIDER WEB

Knowing where the trap is—that's the first step in evading it.

—FRANK HERBERT

Wherever I went, I always got good work because I was *The Italian.* At the time, there weren't many other well-known Italian models in the international circuit—I was one of the few, perhaps even the only one in New York. I got my share of success and had the privilege of working with companies like Armani, Valentino, Just Cavalli, Ermanno Scervino, Costume National, Nike, and so on. I worked with some of the biggest companies and biggest photographers in high fashion. But I never managed to break through the final gateway to ultimate fame because I stopped right on its doorstep.

And now, I'm going to tell you why.

A great photographer is like an artist. He has to have a fine eye, just like someone who creates a statue or a painting. He has to be able to capture an image, a moment, without forcing you into a pose. Lots of photographers say, "Look this way, look that way…" What the hell? You be the photographer, give me a sense of what you want to get, but then let me be the model. That's where my skill comes in.

Being a male or female model isn't just about taking your shirt off in front of a camera. You need to know how to catch the light, how to move. And when you put together a great model and a great photographer, you end up with art, like the work of Steven Klein, Mario Testino, Bruce Weber, or David La Chapelle.

After a casting call in NYC for a "huge" photographer, his studio assistant called me to set up a shoot at his private home in North Miami Beach. It seemed like a dream come true. They flew me down to do a shoot for Vogue, German edition. That was the intent, anyway.

This man was a truly unique and remarkable character. He wasn't the usual photographer who tells you what to do and puts you in prefab poses—I knew this going in. When I arrived, even his house had a character of its own, full of fascinating objects that seemed to tell a story simply when you looked at them.

So, we begin the shoot, and it's not long before he starts getting a little weird. I can clearly tell he's getting all worked up. His breathing gets heavier and heavier as he creepily crawls toward me.

The situation is getting overwhelmingly uncomfortable and incredibly embarrassing. Here I am with someone who had been an icon to me for years, a legend of his craft, a real artist, and now, he's right in front of me. Even before the disappointment crept in, I acknowledged I was at a crossroads. I know that my entire career is at stake, right here, at this very moment.

So, he's coming on to me like that and…

"That's not right. Stop!" I say as I shove him away. "Don't even try it." Then I got up, took my stuff, and walked away.

It's not a matter of being gay or straight—it's a matter of principle. It's a matter of where you draw the line on what you need to do in that situation. Lots of men and women I knew had said, "Yeah, it happened, well, that's the way it goes, it's work…"

Unfortunately, the all-too-common situations of harassment, assault, abuse—they happen everywhere. And I am not criticizing how any victim handles their own situation. I just knew there was only one way to handle my own.

So, I left.

The next day, I go back home to New York, and as soon as I get there, I get a call from one of my bookers. "Would you come into the agency? We need to talk."

"So, tell me. What happened?" he asks abruptly as I step in.

"Well, I don't know really; you tell me what happened," I say. "I'm a professional, and I went there to work, not to compromise myself."

I was about to step into the modeling elite, but after that incident with the photographer, those doors suddenly started closing. From that moment on, it was as if the booker had crossed me, and my career at the top, off his list.

And at that level, the personal relationships were shallow, and it was tough for me to deal with them in the long run. It wore on me, that way of being, "OMG, you're the be-e-est!" one day. The next day, they don't even say hello.

It was harsh. Devastating at times.

No one has any respect for anyone else. That's how it is. You're worth nothing, really.

The main values were lost. The value of the individual person. Sure, it feels nice to make money; it's nice to live a glamorous life. But then you have to face what, and who, that brings along with it.

It's ironic. I had made it to what I thought was "the top," and at the same time, I was the most miserable I'd ever been in my life. A terrible inner sadness seized me.

In fact, that whole world crashed down on me. I felt a huge sense of disappointment inside. I totally lost faith in humanity as a whole.

That whole world had left me with a bitter taste, and this last incident was when I said enough is enough. Well, almost, anyway. When I returned to New York from Miami, I was moving closer to a completely different path.

14.

THE SPIRIT OF THE LION

CALIFORNIA, 2013

So, what do you do then? Do you give up?!

"Wait a second. Am I dreaming?!"

It always happens when I'm cruising downhill that I run into a surprise. I'm popping out fast from behind a ridge when I see this huge, sand-colored cat looking down at me. The moment he realizes I've seen him, he turns and takes off. But I watch where he goes and notice he's just behind a bush, spying on me.

He hadn't run away at all! Those cats just wait for you to pass by and then go for your back. I pick up a rock and stick and proceed slowly, constantly keeping an eye on him. I can see his snout amid the branches, still watching me. I raise my arms to look bigger than I am and show that I'm not afraid. If I run, it might trigger some primordial instinct.

Oh yes, if a mountain lion jumps on you, he'll rip you open. So, I walk slowly, steadily for another fifty yards till I'm around the next bend. Then I tell myself, "Let's go!" And I take off as fast as I possibly can.

What's the expression we use for the most primitive reaction to danger in animals or in humans? Fight or flight. Flight means to run. An animal doesn't run unless it's hunting or being hunted.

Or it's playing.

Little kids play in order to learn how to live. Little lion cubs don't just develop the physical strength of a lion—though that's what we usually think—they also have to develop the lion's *spirit*. If you're down on your back and all you know how to do is surrender, it means you're lacking a very important quality. Because at one point or another, all of us end up down on the ground.

So, what do you do then? Do you give up?!

15.

THE WINDOW ON THE FIFTEENTH FLOOR

MAY, 2009

Sometimes even to live is an act of courage.

—Lucius Annaeus Seneca

I was utterly disappointed and felt like all the hard work, effort, and dedication didn't mean a thing if I wasn't ready to *play the game*. I needed to let loose, and here's where we get to *the* party—my first and last in New York. I'd already taken a couple of slaps to the face at this point. All that was missing was a punch straight in the face to knock me out.

When I'd first arrived in the city, I had done that important photo shoot with Steven Klein, which went really well. He'd invited me to his birthday party at The Standard, a fancy hotel in the Meatpacking District, one of trendiest areas of New York. The party happened to take place the weekend I returned from the horrible incident in Miami. I already sensed that the agency was "crossing me off the list," so I thought, "Why not go to Steven's party? We had a good rapport—maybe I can have a good time and connect with some people who aren't going to take advantage of me?"

Of course, there were the usual rivers of champagne and all those fine things typical of that lifestyle. It was one of those super exclusive parties. There were famous musicians, actors, models, and all Steven Klein's friends from the fashion and movie worlds.

This was the night I met Madonna, who was dating this Brazilian guy, Jesus, at the time. He turned the other way and was doing his own thing when Steven Klein introduced me to her as *Mr. Abs*. So, Madonna, instead of shaking my hand, opens up my shirt and strokes my stomach to make sure I lived up to my nickname, of course.

"My pleasure," she says.

As I turn, a totally wasted guy comes right up to me and whispers, "I want to lick your asshole!"

Gasp! I had just returned from Florida, and now, this? Something inside me snapped. The room and the crowd started to spin—everything was in slow motion as I pushed my way through in silence and left the hotel. It was going to be a cathartic night.

I started walking home because I needed some fresh air. Drunk, I walked along the Hudson River, down the west side, passed Canal Street, and turned by Trinity Church to get to my building. I stepped into the lobby, walked past the doorman at reception, and took the elevator up to the fifteenth floor of my apartment building.

It's quiet when I enter the apartment, and my wife isn't there because she's gone out partying somewhere. Things are pretty much over between us.

I quietly walked into the bathroom and stared at myself in the mirror. "Tonight, I've reached my limit." I spent a really long time there, staring straight into my own eyes, which isn't something I do very often. I watched myself for ten, fifteen, twenty minutes. Once again, in complete silence. I get goose bumps just remembering this.

It's almost dawn as I open the bedroom window and sit on the sill, my legs dangling out the skyscraper's window. I'm out there for a good while. Down below, far away, I see the little red and white lights of the passing cars. And I think...

I sit there, tears pouring down my cheeks, thinking I've lost.

Should I just put an end to it?

I'm on the verge of shouting, "Is this all there is to life?" I'm from a small town of five thousand souls. I've had many unique experiences. I've done everything I could to pursue what's put into our heads as the image of success. The "good life," "parties," "money," and "making it big." I've got it. And in the end, I'm left feeling empty, alone, and adrift.

So, what the hell's the point? I don't get it, *What is the point?*!

This is where I've ended up? I'm twenty-seven years old. I've had everything I wanted. Alone in my room, I open my wallet, pull out my new green card, and tear it up. Enough. Everything I've worked for until now, I reject it. And I sit there...

I've got to decide now. It's time to reevaluate. And then... then my parents came to mind. My sister and all my friends, the people who have always been close to me, and I realize: what a waste it would be. Life is a gift. If you jump, you won't be able to press rewind and go back. They don't deserve this.

I'm still young. I have my whole life ahead of me. I changed the course of the river once; I can do it again.

Right then, I find clarity. I begin to understand the woman I'm with is clearly not for me, and the life I've been living is not for me either.

I need something new. I just don't know what it is yet.

16.

ESCAPE FROM THE CAGE

I want my life to have something extra. I want to feel fulfilled.

—Roz Savage

I was looking for the key that would free me from the cage.

In the meantime, despite everything, work kept coming. I did an underwear campaign, for which I got paid tens of thousands of dollars a day, and there were several days of shooting. That's a huge sum of money for playing a narcissistic, half-naked chump in front of a camera! But it wasn't like before. Fashion was a path to reaching something on my own at the beginning, but I didn't feel the calling to pursue that career any longer. "In thirty to forty years," I thought, "I'll be old and will have lived my life. I'll be sitting down, talking to my child or grandchild, and they'll ask me, 'What did you do in your life?' And all I'll have to say is, 'I guess I showed off my ass in fashion magazines!'"

I kept doing what I was doing. I was still getting high-paying gigs, they just weren't at the elite level I had inadvertently turned down by not letting the "Spider" trap me in his web at the Miami shoot. I guess you could say now I was the "opening band" instead of the headliner on a stadium tour.

I was in the middle of a huge personal crisis, but I kept pressing on. I wasn't happy. I wasn't satisfied. I was desperately looking for something that called me.

And where did I start my search? On the internet, of course. I spent the evenings glued to the computer. Then it came: adventure. Adventure attracted me. In the beginning, more as an escape.

I had a big flat screen and often watched documentaries, almost obsessively, any type I could find. From history to UFOs to religion and exploration—I watched them all.

These things grabbed ahold of me. I started to feel a tinge of emotion.

I read about explorers, adventurers of any kind and watched more and more documentaries and motivational speakers. I started piling up books. Gradually, I found out about a woman who had rowed a boat across the Atlantic Ocean, a man who swam the world's biggest rivers, a man who had climbed the highest mountains, and another man who had crossed the Poles on foot.

I loved the stories of people who just picked up and left on an adventure without thinking of anything but experiencing Nature and the world to their utmost. Experiencing life beyond the cities that keep us chained.

These stories took me outside of my building a bit, beyond the skyscrapers, the streets, the subways, and the crowds. Other people's adventures inspired me. Like the English woman, Roz Savage, who was flipping through the newspaper one day and happened to read an obituary. And as she read who had died that week, she was struck by imagining her own death: husband, two children, a job... Finished. And she said to herself, "I want my life to have something extra. I want to feel fulfilled."

This gave her the inspiration to leave everything behind and put herself on the line. She quit her job, sold her house, bought a rowboat, and started training. Then she crossed the Atlantic Ocean on her own. She started in the Azores and wound up in Antigua in the Caribbean. *Rowing the Atlantic* was a powerful book steeped in the mindset of someone who refused to settle for a life half lived.

Then I came across Martin Strel, the Big River Man, a Slovenian pushing sixty years of age. This guy was not young by any means and sported a bit of a paunch. He inspired me as he was quite out of shape, but thanks to his grit and perseverance, he swam the whole length of some of the longest rivers in the world: the Danube, the Mississippi, the Yangtze, the Amazon.

I read *Endurance* for the first time about the disastrous voyage of Ernest Shackleton to the South Pole. I read about the mountain climbers Reinhold Messner and Walter Bonatti, as well as Bear Grylls' *The Kid Who Climbed Everest*. And then there were the expeditions of Ranulph Fiennes and Alex Bellini, who had decided to tackle two oceans in a rowboat.

The more I scratched at these subjects, the more I learned

and the more they grabbed me. So instead of scratching with my finger, I started digging with my hand. Then with two hands, and before I knew it, I was diving in head first, totally immersed.

To know there were people like this was exciting! I felt this need for extreme adventure—a desire to experience the outdoors. These people did it to pursue their journey. They did it because it was their calling.

I read a book by Lisa Tamati, an Iron Lady from New Zealand who never quits. Together with her boyfriend, another Nature enthusiast, they crossed a piece of the desert in Sudan. They rowed the rugged waters of the Yukon. They crossed half of Europe on bicycles. It was compelling.

I bought new books nearly every week.

In doing all of this reading, a little here and a little there, I came across a guy who set off to circumnavigate the world by human power alone, either in a row boat or on a bicycle. It was then that a spark was ignited in me, and I decided to get on Google Earth to map out the whole route, country by country, city by city, street by street, with great precision. I wrote a list of names and numbers for all the streets with their distances in between. That is, I didn't just mark the countries and the cities but every street in the world! I spent weeks tracing the route. I was so into the idea, every single detail.

I had imagined my route starting from Beijing. I don't know why. I would travel straight to the East to avoid Nepal and the Himalayas. I didn't know if I could go through Afghanistan, so I went up toward Kazakhstan, through all of the Middle East, across Europe, the Strait of Gibraltar, and Morocco. Then I'd take a rowboat from Dakar in Senegal and row to the easternmost point of Brazil. From there, I wouldn't do the Amazon because I'd waste a lot of time, but I'd go north toward Venezuela, Central America, Mexico, the United States, and Canada. Then from Alaska, I'd move into Russia across the Bering Strait, then down toward China to close the circle. It was perfect!

I made myself that absurd map of a tour around the world.

After a while, even when I was going to castings, I took my stuff with me. I would read in the subway. On one occasion, I was the only model for a Valentino fashion room, which is like a private fashion show where new collections are shown directly to corporate clients. I had a seat and a wardrobe, and when they called me to change, I went out and walked around, then changed again and went back out countless times. But every once in a while, I had extended breaks, which meant I had time to read my books and take notes.

One day, I wrote to a Chinese businessman I knew through my father's travels to the East. For some reason, he had stumbled upon *Model Season*, that mini-reality show about models I had done in Miami, and he liked it. He mentioned he had contacts that might be interested in producing something similar in China.

"Why not a reality show about adventure instead of one about fashion?" I suggested to him. Totally out of the blue. "A tour of the world by human power alone. I could even start from Beijing. What do you say?"

I had the desire, although, I still didn't ride a bike, and I certainly didn't know how to row. But none of that mattered to me.

"You're not an athlete or explorer," he answered. "There's little sense to it. You have a long way to go, young man, before setting off on your great adventure."

I had no qualifications. And the thing died right there.

17.

FINDING FREEDOM

AUGUST, 2009

It was a constant search, a labor, an obsession.

In the meantime, I did not surrender. I had my father send me his old road bicycle since he was a cycling enthusiast and had just gotten a brand new one. It was an old Scapin. He sent it to me by mail, and I had to go to customs at the airport to pick it up, as if it were something suspicious.

I started taking that old bike to work and castings, and right away, I felt better about living in the city. I tried to find escape in those rides. I'd cycle through Central Park's greenery and lie down in the Strawberry Fields section.

I watched the clouds pass behind the tree branches.

In New York, I couldn't take the subway any longer—the rancid odors of armpits and people's bad breath in the morning.

At times, it struck me as inhuman to be piled on top of each other like that, like cattle on the way to the slaughterhouse. I needed to hold my breath so the doors could close, we were so squished together. Then the doors closed and *aaaahhh...* You would lean on the others and stay standing without even trying because you'd be packed so tight. Is that any way to live?

Whenever you emerged from the subway into the crowded streets, you'd feel like an ant on an anthill. People walked their paths in every possible direction and somehow never bumped into each other! Then, after a while, you entered into the system and kept pace with the crowd. When I first came to New York, I walked slowly, then I got used to it and kept the pace of an Olympic walker. Because you have to walk from one train to another, from one appointment to another, up and down, here and there, through the whole city.

And it struck me how alone you can feel in a city of eight million people. The loneliness of New York is unlike anywhere else. Each person is absorbed in their own world, with their earbuds and headphones on, looking at their phone or reading on their pads, eyes downward. "I don't know you, and you don't really matter to me." It's awful. A sense of disconnection that always stunned me.

And, as I mentioned before, more and more friends were just fleeting acquaintances. In reality, I was truly alone.

I had discovered so many beautiful stories and exciting adventures, but crossing the ocean in a boat wasn't really for me. Swimming the length of a great river is jaw dropping, but that wasn't for me either. I spent months reading piles of books, watching tons of documentaries, and surfing on the internet for hours on end. It was a constant search, a labor, an obsession.

It took me about a year before I got to the moment in which I said, "That's it! That's what I want to do!!"

18.

THE ULTRAMARATHON MAN

Adventure doesn't necessarily have to be in an exotic place. The adventure starts as soon as you plunge into anything where the outcome is unknown.

In the meantime, that winter, I decided to sign up for the New York Film Academy. Maybe acting would give me new momentum.

That's where I met Lauren. It was instant, an attraction at first sight. A spark, an immediate connection, and within a short time, we started a platonic relationship. Initially as friends, we went out together with other people from our classes; at times, there were thirty to forty of us. It was a very special time. We shared the pleasure of going to the movies or eating out, seeing each other, and simply spending time together. There were clearly feelings between us, but I came out clean right away, "My situation is quite difficult at the moment," I told her. "I am in the middle of a deep crisis, and you know, I'm married." In the end, though, we kissed anyway.

She was the sweetest girl I'd ever met. Simply gorgeous with an outstanding sense of humor and a certain class. In many ways, she helped me regain my trust in people and in relationships, too. With her, I took the reins back in my hands, retraced my steps back to my values, and started breathing easy again.

My heart was finally finding contentment, though I was still looking for a personal change that would fill me with spirit.

It took almost a whole year. During the Christmas holiday of 2010, I had a date with Lauren at our favorite Thai restaurant near Union Square. I was waiting there as it started to snow. It was cold. So, I jumped into the giant Barnes & Noble on the north end of the square and headed straight for the sports section, looking for yet another adventurous read, when...

My eyes fell on the cover of a book. An action-figure-type guy with thick, muscular legs jumped out from under the title: ULTRAMARATHON MAN. In bold letters. "Who is this guy?" I eagerly picked up the book, turned it around, and read the first page. Then two, three, four. Wow! I devoured nearly half the book while waiting. I bought it, and that night, I finished it. My goodness, there was something in the book that grabbed hold of me on a deep level. I reread it from the beginning, and then read it again a third time that week. Though our paths were different, I saw a lot of myself in what the author shared in his story.

A new horizon opened up ahead. "This might be what I'm looking for!"

I got the urge to run again. Not just to stay in shape. But to start a new journey.

Not just to run a few miles but to run an ultra. An ultramarathon is a race that's longer than a marathon, often much longer. "Run when you can, walk if you have to, crawl if you must; just never give up," wrote Dean Karnazes. And he inspired me. I was thirsty for new experiences, and I wanted to push myself past my known boundaries. I wanted to see what these ultras were all about.

The challenges described by Karnazes were so long and arduous they became voyages in themselves. He recounted how he discovered the Western States Endurance Run, a one-hundred-mile race that originated as a horse race. In 1974, a tall man by the name of Gordy Ainsleigh decided to race against horses and ended up beating some of them. Incredible! After that impressive debut, they decided to hold the race every year in the mountains but for humans, and the race became famous. One hundred miles—four marathons back to back. Karnazes wrote about it as if it were the ultimate challenge.

Adventure doesn't necessarily have to be in an exotic place. The adventure starts as soon as you plunge into anything where the outcome is unknown.

I had to start somewhere.

"OK," I tell myself. "Tomorrow is New Year's Day. As of tomorrow, I'll start training. I want to run one hundred miles, too."

19.

THE REAL MARATHON

...the real challenge now is to find out how far we can actually go. It becomes absolute. And that's where you transcend all ancient tales or cultural preconceptions. In the past, we gave ourselves limits. Now, we're discovering we can always go beyond.

There are roughly twenty-five miles between Marathon and Athens, and that was supposed to be the distance of the new challenge, the "marathon," which Pierre de Coubertin launched during the first modern Olympics in 1896. But it so happened that during the 1908 Olympics in London, the Queen of England wanted her children to see the start from their window in Windsor Castle. From the castle to the stadium, the distance was exactly twenty-six miles and 385 yards, and to this day, that remains the official length of the marathon.

In the first years after its invention, the marathon was one of the most popular and dramatic events of the Olympic games.

The end of the 1908 race in particular remains one of the most exciting moments in athletic history. The first runner to reach the stadium in London amid the thundering applause of one hundred thousand spectators was a little Italian man named Dorando Pietri. But at this point, he was so exhausted that he staggered about and, in the attempt to complete the last lap in the stadium, fell four times. Some people came to help him for the final meters and held him up to reach the finish line, but because of this help, he was disqualified. Originally in second place, the American J.J. Hayes was declared the winner. Nonetheless, Pietri became an international celebrity.

The epic event that inspired the modern race was the exploit of a poor Greek messenger, Pheidippides, in the sixth century BC. After having run nonstop from Marathon to the Acropolis to announce the Athenian people's victory over the Persians, Pheidippides died. That story, however, is incomplete. Because the messenger didn't die as a result of running that handful of miles. No, Pheidippides' real exploit was that shortly before the invasion of the Persians, he—as a *hemerodromos*, a military courier—had been sent by the Athenians to ask the Spartans for help. He ran 145 miles to Sparta, which was a city-state at the time. He got a nice, "No thanks; it's your problem" from the king as a reply. The following day, Pheidippides had to run back to Athens. So, he covered almost three hundred miles round trip in three days with the added weight of bad news.

Wait, that's not the end of it.

The Athenian army was then sent to Marathon to fight against the soldiers of Persia's King Darius, who seriously outnumbered them. Yet, miraculously, they won. Pheidippides, who, as a soldier, had just fought against the Persians, was sent running back to Athens again to announce the victory. "Rejoice! We've won!" he manages to say. So, basically, he'd run three hundred miles round trip, fought in a battle, and then run a marathon back to Athens to bring the news. No shit he died!

That's the story that few people know, though.

When the modern Olympics were created, de Coubertin launched the idea of the marathon as some kind of ultimate challenge. That was the limit of what was humanly possible: twenty-six miles. Because, as the story went, the first poor soul to run that distance had died, so it seemed like going beyond that limit would be fatal.

Today, we've obliterated the barrier of the marathon. There are people who are perfectly capable of running four, five, six, or seven marathons in a row. Without stopping. In fact, the marathon is hardly even considered a long race anymore. For these new athletes, it's a sustained sprint, much like a 5K or 10K race. If you want to run a marathon, fine, go ahead. But the real challenge now is to find out how far we can actually go. It becomes absolute. And that's where you transcend all ancient tales or cultural preconceptions. In the past, we gave ourselves limits. Now, we're discovering we can always go beyond.

This is what fascinates me.

20.

THE FIRST STEP IS THE HARDEST

NEW YORK, 2011

The secret of getting ahead is getting started.

—MARK TWAIN

The most difficult step of any journey is the first one—the one you take out of your front door, so they say. The day after New Year's 2011, I took that first step and went into the sporting goods store, bought some awful minimalist shoes, and put them on, taking the step to move forward from doing little "jogs" with my model friends to seriously advancing my training.

Right away, I jumped in. I wanted to experience the challenge and the exhilaration that Karnazes talked about. I had to find myself a one-hundred-mile race. Why not? He'd been able to do it. If I'm dissatisfied, why can't I change my life and try something new?

That's when I found out about the Keys 100.

It was perfect. The race took place in Florida, not far from Miami. At least it would be in a warm place, and I'd enjoy the experience in the gorgeous setting.

I signed up immediately. Now, I had a goal.

I had a little less than five months to prepare. Five months?! Obviously, a training plan was important from the get-go—the leisurely jogs with my model friends weren't going to cut it anymore. Once again, I tapped into the internet to do some research and read lots of articles and blogs until I landed on the site of Anton Krupicka. *Riding the Wind.* It pulled me right in.

I saw his photos. He was an inspiring character, a clear image of freedom, with his long hair and wild beard, often running without even a T-shirt through the high mountains of Colorado. He represented the sport in its purest form. He rode around in his truck, where he slept when he was out looking for new peaks to explore. That was his world, his life-style. Krupicka represented the joy of running free in Nature and absorbing energy from the Earth. That was his message, or at least, that's what I perceived. He posted fantastic images of the places where he ran and climbed, and he spoke of his adventures in an enthralling way, too.

He immediately became a reference point for me. At the time, you could find on YouTube a documentary called *Indulgence: 1,000 Miles Under the Colorado Sky.* Cool, right? And it's about this guy, Krupicka, who in the five weeks before a one-hundred-mile race ran some two hundred miles a week up and down the Rocky Mountains. I thought, "How the hell does he do it?!" He ran a gargantuan number of miles, which many at the time thought was excessive and counterproductive.

But in the meantime, he ran all those miles and noticed his fitness level increased more while having fun in the mountains than when doing drills on the track. In fact, he went on to win several big one-hundred-mile races and many others, too. He became a star in the world of ultra running. Noticing his excellent results and not really knowing anyone else who ran such distances, I said to myself, "OK, if he's this good, I'll copy his plan and train like he does, so I'll be good, too." Doesn't that make total sense?

At the time, he kept a blog that was practically a training log. He wrote every day of the week in minute detail. So, I studied it. Clearly, I couldn't start at 160 miles per week, which was his average at the time. I had to build up to that distance gradually. I started with a base of fifteen miles per week, then slowly worked my way up to thirty, fifty, eighty, one hundred, one hundred twenty, one hundred forty miles…Week after week, month after month. I used Krupicka as a role model and followed his example. So, in the span of four and a half months, right before the race, I finally got to a training load of about 160 miles per week like Krupicka—even if it was pretty reckless.

"I'll just do it and see what happens."

I did all my preparations in the cold of New York City, which meant snow, freezing rain, and wind, but no matter the weather, I put on my shoes and went out to run. At times, it was well below zero, but I didn't skip a single training session. I was fully committed. "This is what I want to do, so this is what I *have* to do," I said to myself. And I did it.

You need consistency to give your body time to change, to reinvent yourself. You can't do it overnight. So, I made sure to punch in every single day.

* * *

During the longest training sessions, I carried ten dollars in my pocket and ran a loop around Manhattan, winding up at the bottom of the island and then maybe getting some take-out food in Chinatown before going back home. Or I'd stop at the food trucks at the entrance to Central Park, under the statue of Columbus, where they sold soft drinks, ice creams, muffins, stuff like that. After a while, the vendors in the kiosks got to know me, and when I passed by, they'd often offer me a muffin or a treat.

A few times, I literally arrived there on my knees because I'd pushed myself too far. One day, after one of those long training sessions, I went with some friends to train at the gym, and while I was warming up on the treadmill, *bammm!* I blacked out. They carried me like dead weight back into my apartment; I couldn't manage to wake up. I was lying down on the couch like a corpse. Fortunately, one of them got the idea of squeezing a packet of honey into my mouth, and thanks to that energetic nectar, I slowly came back to my senses.

I was still very much living in two worlds—the adventures I sought had taken me on a five-month journey to a one-hundred-mile race. Yet, I still wasn't able to leave fashion—I leaned on it for income. As much as I wanted to jump head-first into running, I couldn't turn down making money in my livelihood at the time. And, in one sense, wasn't the misery of the fashion industry what allowed me to find my new path and passion for running?

21.

THE TOP OF THE MOUNTAIN

SUMMER, 2014

Go to the top of the mountain and look around.
If you don't like what you see, you can always come back.
But if you like it, keep going. Go and see what's beyond.

—CESARE GRAGLIA

You can't just stay in a cage. You have to live life and be open to every new experience. And you can't always be perfect. You have to try different paths to see what works and what doesn't. Even if you fall, it doesn't matter. You can easily process the difficult moments and defeats. In any case, life goes on, and if today was bad, tomorrow will be better. Learn, grow, move forward. There's no point in dwelling on the past.

That's what I was taught. My father always pushed me to go a step further. He's the one who sent me to Japan when I turned twenty-one to attend a trade fair and find new clients. He was also the one who encouraged my idea of moving to the United States, even if that meant the major sacrifice of not seeing his son for long periods of time.

My parents always told me, "Go to the top of the mountain and look around. If you don't like what you see, you can always come back. But if you like it, keep going. Go and see what's beyond."

Climbing up to the top of a mountain allows you to see the world from a different perspective. Now, I really get to explore the mountains, keep going, and see what's beyond. I can wander around to different parks, climb here, train there, cross paths with Nature. I only go back down because I have a home to return to—a home I want to return to. For a long time, I craved that feeling. To explore beyond and not have to go back to a daily life that was killing me inside.

I'd never move back to New York. I'd go visit if I had to, but I couldn't see myself living there again. Those were three very uncomfortable years. Life was too tight for me in that city. The noise of the traffic, the herds of people, the chaos of daily life. I chose to get away and go to the great outdoors, leave things behind, and lose myself in Nature, running alone. That's when I'm happiest.

* * *

One of the most memorable experiences I had was in the summer of 2014 just before the Angeles Crest 100. I was somewhat already training at altitude in the San Gabriel mountains or up in Big Bear Lake, but to really tune up my body, I decided to go up to Mount Whitney, the highest mountain in the contiguous United States. It's about a three-and-a-half-hour drive from Los Angeles. So, one Friday morning, I packed my car and left. I was hoping to go for a day and a night. The permits to climb Whitney were very restricted, and there's even a lottery at the beginning of the year to get them. However, sometimes people don't show up, so if you're there in person, they might give you one of the unused permits.

There was a smiling young lady at the Park Ranger's office.

"How many permits do you need?"

I paused. "What do you mean, how many?"

She blinked back and reiterated. "How many permits do you need?"

"Uh…" I gulped. "Three, I guess."

What luck! Now I could stay for *three days* in this paradise! I'd brought my food supply, a few changes of clothing, and my running shoes, of course. But on the first day, I got to the trailhead late and slept in the car at the portals. Then, at 4:30 a.m., I woke up and started running with only a water bottle in hand, determined to get to the top of Mount Whitney.

Along the trail, I come across a few hikers. They were classic walkers with big boots and huge backpacks over their shoulders looking like they were moving homes. What on earth are they carrying? I wondered. It seemed like they were about to go on an expedition in the Himalayas for two weeks. All high-tech, kitted out with hiking poles, crampons, pots, and tubes that carried water from their backs to their mouths.

It's about eleven miles uphill, going from an altitude of 8,500 to 14,500 feet above sea level. In the beginning, the trail climbs beneath these tall firs, then the trees become sparser, you pop out of the woods, and everything becomes rockier. You get to a big gorge, find a lake, then continue. There's another glacier lake, then the climb gets steeper and steeper until it gets to a final plateau, looking out onto a series of massive rock faces.

It's STUNNING. Then begins a series of switchbacks up the rock walls that bring you to a crest where you take the John Muir Trail and run along the entire ridge.

Finally, I'm at the summit of Mount Whitney!

Admiration for the beauty of Nature is something we all have in common. There's no getting around it. Whether it's the sea or the desert, the forest, a glacier, or tundra, the world is beautiful. It gives us so many primal sensations. Smells, colors, rays of sunlight cutting through the clouds. That's where we find the connection to Nature. Climbing up the mountain makes us understand how insignificant we are, and the experience is so humbling it allows us to appreciate the world in its entirety even more.

We tend to give ourselves too much importance sometimes, and at the same time, we develop a fear of what we don't know and of what's different from ourselves. Nature is not a monster; it's our friend. And it's not even absurd to think of it as a loving Mother. We were born and raised on the Earth, where we continue to live. It must never be feared, but rather, it should be known and appreciated. It's our home after all!

Seen from up here, the temporal arc of four and a half billion years in which the Earth has been spinning, with the evolution of man going on for only the past two hundred thousand years—a blink in comparison—I find it hard to believe in our credos and convictions at times or to put any stake in our economies, religions, and borders.

Nature is our goddess. The Earth breathes just as we and all the other animals do. If only we could learn to see *her* as an entity not to be usurped but rather to be venerated. To be listened to, not subjugated. To be lived. It's not a war. It's a quest to ultimately come to know ourselves and reach a higher understanding of our place in relationship to *her*.

At the summit of this mountain, I feel the wind caressing my face. It's an invigorating feeling. I feel so alive. It's not a secret formula—it's like this for everyone who comes here.

My thoughts are focused as I live in the moment and move unbounded.

It's an opportunity to detach from the outside world and confront ourselves, our deepest thoughts and fears. Step after step, breath after breath. Because it's only when we find ourselves in the rawest of conditions, reaching for that physical limit, that we discover our true strength and resilience. Past pain, past suffering. Seeking ultimate freedom, tapping into our unadulterated mind, and giving voice to our purest self, our true essence.

Contemplating the truths of our very own existence in

the profound knowledge that man actualizes himself at his highest level.

And when you realize that, well, everything else simply becomes secondary.

Whether you're a climber, a surfer, scuba diver, trail runner, hiker, snowboarder, or whatever else, there's that underlying feeling.

We sense the need to get closer to Nature. In fact, it's for this reason that more and more people are embracing running. Trail running, ultra trails, and ultra running are literally exploding. This growth is born out of an increasing need to break out of that cage. Running is simply a means, and it's so simple that anyone can do it. You put on a pair of sneakers and go running or hiking. Or maybe you don't even bother with the shoes. Just go. The essential point is to start!

We need to rediscover ourselves in the joy of living in the moment and do something that reconnects us to the energy from which we were born.

Even though we may fear and often resist it, we need change. Change is necessary for evolution and survival. And it's in moments of crisis that we evolve. We can all agree with this. Our society at present is clearly experiencing challenging times. It's understood that the world is suffering, and we are suffering from our very own lifestyles.

I find it intriguing that surfers more or less even answer the same way when asked, "Why do you spend your days outside?" They play with the ocean. They want to be in the sun, in the open air. That's what makes them feel connected and at peace.

It's no surprise. They say surfers and ultra runners are some of the happiest people on the planet.

Are you depressed? Get moving! If the body is in movement, the mind can't be depressed. It's possible to live sports as a means of getting out in Nature. At the top of Mount Whitney, I take off my shoes and really feel the energy of the Earth. I absorb that energy even when I have my shirt off in the sun.

Man, do I feel ecstatic!

After the summit, I head another eleven miles downhill to get back to the car. I find it entertaining as I run up and down and encounter people who are somewhat bewildered and eager to take a picture with me while exchanging a few words. They just cannot process that someone could run on that type of terrain and at that elevation.

"What are you doing? But why?? And how?!"

In between a few pictures and some laughs, I get back to the trailhead. I leave before breakfast and make it back down for lunch. I eat; rest up a bit; put on the backpack in which I have my little blue tent, a sleeping bag, and some food; and I start running back up to the twelve-thousand-foot camp. Another six miles and four thousand feet higher. This is the kind of training I set out to do and was free to run as much as I wanted. I stop next to the last high lake, right under the summit. I put up the tent and go with my filter to suck some water out of the creek and into my pouch. That night, at twelve thousand feet, I sleep like a rock.

In the morning, I wake up and head straight out to climb to the summit of Whitney then run back all the way down to the car for lunch. Again. By now, it's early afternoon. I could have been done right then, but I have the urge to go back up to the top once more, running past my tent on my way to the summit for the third time in two days. Though, as I begin the climb, I notice huge black clouds coming my way from behind the ridge.

The wind quickly kicks up as I feel the first drops on my skin. Then suddenly, rain and sleet start coming down. I took off from the trailhead in a pretty minimalist way, wearing just a pair of short shorts and a flimsy windbreaker. I'm less than two miles from the top. Hmmm…tough decision. What do I do?

If I get caught by a storm up there, I'll never get back down, so I come to my senses. I turn around and head back downhill.

I barely have enough time to dive into my tent at high camp when the downpour starts. The wind is hitting so violently that my tent starts blowing around left and right, and the only reason it doesn't fly away is because I'm in it. Shortly after the sun sets behind the ridge line, it turns bitter cold. I'm shivering and shaking uncontrollably. "You came unprepared, and now, you have to pay the price," I keep scolding myself. "If you'd simply brought a nice jacket and a pair of pants, you'd be fine. Maybe a pair of gloves would have been nice, too, actually!"

Outside, it's still storming. I can't even unzip the tent to go out and take a leak. Good thing the tent has a little zipper on the side, which serves as my go-to bathroom in case of emergency. Alone in a tent at twelve thousand feet, I slip into the sleeping bag and fortunately, after a little while inside, it starts to get warm.

It's six thirty in the evening. I stayed in the tent the whole night under that storm without even sticking my nose outside. It rained hard for fourteen hours straight. Imagine lying like that the whole time in a tiny tent, practically like a corpse in a coffin! Through the absurdity of it all, I reckoned these adventures during training are often more exciting than the race itself. You experience solitude—an enjoyable solitude—and you come to confront and experience the true majesty and force of Nature directly.

I brought Henry David Thoreau's *Walden* with me, a classic of American philosophy, which I read with the light of my headlamp. "I went to the woods because I wished to live deliberately, to front only the essential facts of life, and see if I could not learn what it had to teach, and not, when I came to die, discover that I had not lived…"

While reading, I chew on some cranberries that a hiker along the trail had kindly offered me earlier. "*Go confidently in the direction of your dreams! Live the life you've imagined.*"

Wind and lightning break out on all sides. The tent sways some more as I lie there, reading Thoreau and listening to the raindrops.

I fall asleep at times, but then *ba-booomm!* Some lighting hits nearby and the thunder wakes me up like a deafening alarm.

At eight o'clock in the morning, the sound of thunder seems to cease for a bit. I peek outside and: "C'mon, c'mon, c'mon! Now's my chance. If I don't go now, I might miss this window." So, I change up really quick, jump outside, fold up my sleeping bag, and take down the tent.

As I'm loading up the backpack, I hear another lightning strike: *booommm!* right behind me as it starts raining again. I'm screwed. Yesterday, I was running without a T-shirt, and now, there's wind and rain and it's practically freezing. "What do I do now?" I'm shaking like a leaf. Hypothermia is a horrible thing. I've felt it several times in the mountains, but never like this. With every second that passes, I'm getting rained on more and more, and before I realize it, I'm completely drenched. Now, even if I take all my stuff out of the backpack, pitch the tent, and go inside, I'm soaked, and I'll certainly freeze to death right on the spot.

So, I do the most sensible thing I can do at that moment: I start running!

I start charging downhill as I run my ass off. At least I'll get warm. I rush headlong down the mountain. It's raining so hard the trail becomes a river that comes up to my calves in places—*chaff, chaff, chaff.* I see lightning bolts strike here and there in the valley. But I keep running. At least I'm going for it. If lightning strikes me, it's too bad. But if I stop, then I'm a goner for sure!

At one point, I pass by some huge boulders and hear a shout. "Come here! Come, take shelter!! Quick!!!"

Down below, there's a group of hikers all kitted out with their rain jackets, long pants, and gloves. I keep charging, half naked:

"I can't, otherwise I'll freeze and diiiiieeee!" I shout loudly as I buzz by.

I descend about three thousand feet before getting under

the thick forest canopy, where the temperature is already a bit more bearable. When I finally get to the car, I turn the heat on full blast, take my clothes off, and sit still for an hour. Half in disbelief, I'm so thankful I made it down all in one piece.

I'm still alive! And I now consider that to be one of the most beautiful experiences I've ever had. I stepped out of my safety bubble and felt the true force of Nature with all her might.

22.

PLUS ULTRA!

I am the master of an empire on which the sun never sets.

—King Charles V

Hercules was the strongest of the Greek heroes. Son of the god Zeus and a mortal woman, he was so strong that no man or mythological monster could ever defeat him. In the end, he had to set himself on fire to die. They say that apart from being the protector of athletes and gyms, he was also the founder of the Olympic Games.

During his famous twelve feats—in which he had to confront a lion, a ferocious boar, a hydra with nine heads, a flock of birds with iron feathers, and even had to follow a female deer that ran as fast as an arrow for an entire year—the hero reached the limits of the world. There, he came upon a mountain and split it in two. He inscribed the words *NON PLUS ULTRA*. Literally, "No more beyond."

The Pillars of Hercules in the Strait of Gibraltar where the Mediterranean Sea ends and the Atlantic Ocean opens marked the limits of the known world, beyond which no mortal could venture.

Time passed. When the Trojan War was won, another hero, Ulysses, set sail for home, his beloved Ithaca. What was supposed to be a simple voyage of return, however, turned into a legendary "Odyssey," during which he encountered all sorts of obstacles and watched all his boats sink and all his men die. In the end, Ulysses was the only one who reached Ithaca, where he had immense joy in reuniting with his wife and son. His old dog, Argo, was so happy to see his master as he had waited so long, he was finally able to die in peace. And yet, after a few years of life at home, surrounded by family and friends in the ease of his own palace, Ulysses, now old but still desirous of knowledge, decided to leave once again for one last "mad voyage."

This time, he sailed across the entire Mediterranean, toward the point at the end of the world where the sun sets, to the famous pillars still standing with Hercules' warning: *NON PLUS ULTRA.*

So, what did Ulysses do? "Oh, brothers…" he shouted, turning to his companions. It was a moment so important it inspired Dante to write one of his most famous verses: "Consider your seed: you were not made to live as brutes, but to follow knowledge and virtue."

And so, they went—onwards, ever onwards. They left the shores of the known and plunged into the endless, blue ocean. Beyond the Pillars of Hercules…

ULTRA!!!

More time passed. Christopher Columbus, born in Genoa, went to work for Portugal's merchant navy, which was the greatest at the time, and became an expert in winds and currents. On many occasions, he sailed the coast of Western Europe and down to Africa, but no one had dared to cross the great ocean yet. Or, if someone had tried, like Ulysses, he never came back to tell his story.

Columbus gradually got the idea that by sailing westward he could reach the Orient, the lands of India and China. But the Portuguese weren't interested in his idea, and even Spain's nautical experts were skeptical at first. But finally, favored by Queen Isabella, the expedition was financed.

Like Ulysses before him, Christopher Columbus left the coast and set sail on what seemed like a sea without an end. No one knew for certain what was on the other side or if there was anything at all. Even though they didn't agree with his calculations of distance, the greatest cartographers of his time suspected there must be a marine route that continued toward the Orient. Everyone was wrong. Even Columbus. But the courage of his endeavor led to a greater discovery: another previously unknown continent that lay between Europe's west coast and the farthest eastern reaches of Asia—a New World that for hundreds of years represented hope, riches, and the unlimited potential of the human spirit.

The discovery that Columbus made while pushing across the unknown ocean changed the fate of Spain, which in a short span of time became a world power so vast that Charles

V, grandson of the same Queen Isabella who had financed Columbus, said, "I am the master of an empire on which the sun never sets."

On the emperor's coat of arms, there are two pillars symbolizing man's physical and mental limits. Between the pillars is his personal motto, which became the motto of Spain, an exhortation to risk and go beyond all possible limits: *PLUS ULTRA*.

23.

CONSUMED

MAY, 2011

It's a return to our roots. It's all connected. And the more you practice [nutrition], the more you see everything is connected. Everything has a meaning.

It would have been easy to give up. I could have quit right after the Keys 100. I fell flat on my face and did quite a bit of damage. The day after that race, I was laid out on the bed with blood flowing from my wounds, which had opened from chafing.

I couldn't get out of bed. I was completely depleted. I couldn't even eat because my stomach was destroyed. I'd run until I couldn't run another step—one more step could have been the difference between life and death.

Still, I believed I could have made it. That's the philosophy of the ultra: never give up, no matter what, and keep going until you reach your goal. What happens in the middle shouldn't concern you. Fall flat today? Don't worry; you'll get back up and make it tomorrow. Many times, you hear people say, "It didn't go so well. This is obviously not for me." No, you figure out where you went wrong and then improve.

Right? No one is born "knowing" everything already.

Failure is simply an obstacle on the path to success. You may not win your first race, and in my case, I didn't even finish my first race. But you get up and continue on the path you've chosen. Failing doesn't mean you're a failure if you overcome the obstacle and continue on the path.

And so, with that conviction lurking in my mind, I spent a day and a half in bed, then Mom, Dad, and Lauren carried me out to the car, skin and bones, all beat up. Perhaps physically broken, but not emotionally.

On the drive from the Keys back to Miami, I even had to carve enough energy to go to the courthouse so I could sign my divorce papers from that previous disastrous relationship. Given the tight schedule and my limited mobility, I almost missed my flight back to NYC. I was practically unable to walk to the gate. Despite the physical pain, though, that last step to end my marriage was a huge relief.

Now I could live my relationship with Lauren out in the open. We got an apartment and moved in together.

It took me two months to get back to walking normally. Forget about running.

"Ok," I said to myself. "Now figure out what you did wrong."

With the Keys 100, I realized nutrition was fundamental.

And what did I know about nutrition? Nothing. Nothing at all.

Now I know I was practically eating myself alive having pushed myself to such an extreme limit without replenishing my salts and nutrients. If you don't replenish fats, you take it from your fat reserves, and that's fine. If you need calcium, you take it from your bones. And if you need magnesium, zinc, or potassium? You get it from your cartilages, from your tendons. If you don't replenish proteins, you take it straight from your muscles. And obviously, that's not good. You virtually start to cannibalize yourself. Instead of the ouroboros, with the serpent eating its own tail, here we have the phenomenon of the runner eating his own legs.

Obviously, I had made some major mistakes. As soon as I realized what they were, I came to the conclusion I needed to expand my knowledge in the area of nutrition and study personal training and fitness. Not necessarily just for running but for my overall well-being. I had to learn physiology, hydration, sports nutrition, and so on. It was an extraordinary process of discovery that involved a lot of research and experimenting on myself.

When I worked in fashion, I had no concept of nutrition, really.

Models, female models in particular, have a fairly simple diet: no food. But this diet is neither sustainable nor healthy. To run long distances, you need sustenance—real fuel. Simply limiting food intake is wrong, so I had to change my approach.

Too often, you hear people say, "Yeah, I went on a diet, but two months later, I gained the weight back." As a reaction to restriction, our bodies have a tendency to overcompensate, and we end up right back where we started.

We've all heard of the food pyramid. These guidelines came out in the 1970s, recommending a diet of around 70 percent carbohydrates, 20 percent protein, and 10 percent fat. We were always taught we needed to eat this way.

But what if we try something new, something radical?

What if we flip the pyramid upside down?

There's a hypothesis, a new philosophy that's currently revolutionizing the world of endurance sports nutrition. I don't want to sound like a conspiracy theorist, but surely the food industry has gone in the direction of cheap and easily produced food (often full of sugar and cornstarch, which create addiction). Pasta, bread, and potatoes all cost little money, but they simply fill your belly rather than giving you nutrients.

I, like many other athletes, have tried to move to a diet that limits these simple carbohydrates: a pseudo-paleo diet, if you will, which is inspired by the diet of original Paleolithic humans in the Stone Age.

The idea of this diet is derived from a fascinating line of thought.

At one point in history, we were hunter-gatherers. You grabbed berries off the bush and fruit off the tree, pulled carrots out of the ground, hunted animals, picked mushrooms, and gathered leaves and seeds. That was how we fed ourselves. Pasta and bread didn't exist then, obviously. These foods appeared only after the agricultural revolution some ten thousand years ago, when our way of life became more sedentary and we stopped moving from place to place in order to cultivate the earth.

But originally, for hundreds of thousands of years, humans fed on a wide variety of very nutritious foods. And according to some researchers, the grains we domesticated and now sow in vast fields have increased the quantity of food at our disposal but not the quality. Primitive man was stronger.

Simple, right?

There are many variations to this approach, one of which is low in carbohydrates and rich in fats, now referred to as "Optimized Fat Metabolism" (OFM). Some recommend a lot of meat, whereas I hardly eat meat at all. In any case, nutrition should be rethought and experimented with depending on each person and their individual needs. But one thing is certain now: what our grandparents used to say is not true. They used to believe that eating a lot of meat made you strong, powerful. "Meat makes good blood!" as they would say in Italy. Or "You become all weak and pale if you only eat vegetables." Weak?! You must be kidding!

In the world of ultra running, a sport that requires extreme endurance, there's a particularly illuminating example that challenges the idea of eating meat. Scott Jurek is, without a doubt, one of the greatest all-around ultra runners alive. He's had success on roads, in the mountains, uphill, downhill; wherever you put him, he's succeeded. He's a universal athlete. The interesting thing about Scott Jurek is that he's not just a vegetarian. He's a vegan. And he's not an outstanding runner *despite* being vegan, he is an outstanding runner *because* he is vegan.

I am not fully vegan, I just choose to eat foods that are simple, natural, and, as far as possible, unprocessed. That means, first, loads of fresh, raw vegetables. I'll graze on salad portions that seem like they're made for a horse for half an hour. Not lettuce, which has practically the same nutritional value as air, but dark green leaves: spinach, arugula, and kale, all highly nutritious. Sweet potatoes, tomatoes, carrots, cucumbers, zucchini, and some mushrooms. They're all carbohydrates but complex carbohydrates. A few eggs here and there. Avocados. Fruit, especially berries. Almonds, walnuts, and seeds. Everything that is very colorful. Sometimes, I'll eat a little fish, especially salmon, for its fat, mostly. Very little though. And I completely avoid refined sugar (except for during ultras, as you'll come to find out).

Sugar is a simple carbohydrate and highly addictive. Pasta, rice, snacks, potato chips, candies, all these packaged things are full of it. Hence, the constant desire to have more. A single can of Coca-Cola contains three days' worth of an adult's daily sugar requirement. A week's worth of the sugar requirement for a child. After the kids go to a birthday party with cake, ice cream, and soda, they should go without another grain of sugar for three months!

Most of my nutrients now come from good fats. Fat has constantly been depicted as bad, but in reality, it's what allows us to survive and thrive. Fat is not an enemy—it's vital, actually, especially when it comes to endurance. It's what allows us to go further, to go beyond. It does this by adapting the body, so it uses its lipid metabolism, teaching it to burn its fat reserves instead of looking for sugars and carbohydrates.

This process of readapting the body to burn fat requires a commitment in the first weeks because you go through periods of debilitating fatigue, but when you get through, there's no falling into the pattern of "turning back." It truly becomes a habit.

It's fantastic when you begin to understand the mechanisms of your body. You no longer have the sustenance of carbohydrates that give you a glycemic spike and then two or three hours later, you're hungry again or need a coffee with sugar to make it to the end of the day. Instead, you have a constant release of energy all day long. You feel better; you're livelier. This is something that transcends sports and can be applied in everyday life.

I've experimented with the low-carb diet and have seen that eating this way has brought me improved results. But it involves constant research and adjustment.

I believe that some form of this combination will trailblaze the guidelines for the proper human diet of the future.

Nowadays, I wake up in the morning and go running, often without eating anything at all. I just drink a glass of water, and I'm out the door. In life in general, I'm more lucid and clear-headed and have more vitality. I feel like jumping all the time. At the level of athletic performance, you have a nearly inexhaustible reserve of energy because even a very thin person has enough fuel in them to run one hundred miles without ever needing to replenish if they're metabolically adapted!

The big secrets are nutrition and adaptation.

Just like the act of running is, in a certain sense, a return to the primordial state, your diet can also bring you back to a mode of eating more naturally. It's an ethical question of sustainability, connection to our planet, and respecting other living beings. It's a return to our roots. It's all connected. And the more you practice it, the more you see everything is connected. Everything has a meaning.

24.

VICTORY

SUMMER, 2011

He who says he can and he who says he can't are both usually right.

—Confucius

Lauren and I left NYC for South Florida and warmer weather. I started training again at the end of that summer. It was three months from the time I wrecked myself. After the Keys, something happened to my tendons and everything else—I had inflammation so severe that whatever shoes I wore gave me problems. It hurt here, it hurt there, my knee was sore deep inside, my hip bothered me no matter how I moved, my ankles, my tendons, even the ball of my foot; I had excruciating pain all over. And one thing was for sure, I couldn't find a pair of shoes that fit me. I'd bought four pairs of running shoes, different brands, different types. I put on one pair, and something hurt; I put on another pair, and something else hurt. Each time, the problem moved. Every shoe gave me a different set of issues. So, for a while, I ran barefoot. On the streets, in the park, downtown, everywhere barefoot. I even created a small running group in my community, and ten or fifteen of us got together once or twice a week to run.

Eventually, my body slowly realigned itself. I spent a few months focused on training again, and at the end of February 2012, eight months after the Keys 100, I signed up for the Everglades 50. A fifty-miler this time. Half the distance of my previous race.

The Everglades 50 takes place in the Florida swamps and passes through the same wild wetlands I saw when I first arrived by plane from Italy. It was kind of an adventure and definitely nostalgic, which piqued my interest. We were in the Fakahatchee Strand Preserve State Park, the wildest of the Everglades preserves, where it is completely undeveloped. You enter this national park where pumas and alligators roam freely. You actually see alligators everywhere. I even stopped to take a photo of a few of them from above.

In Florida, the relationship between man and Nature is still pretty wild. A woman I knew ended up in the newspapers because she'd stopped to tie her shoelaces near a canal by her house when an alligator came up quietly from behind, grabbed her, and pulled her into the water. She never came back up.

Some of the sections we ran involved crossing streams with water up to our knees. I wound up in a part that looked like a savannah, and at one point, I turned and saw a herd of deer running beside us. Such an amazing experience.

From there, I pushed ahead and moved into the top ten, and at one point, about halfway through the race, I saw the leader not far ahead and slowly caught up to him. We introduced ourselves and talked a bit as we went along. We clicked right away and ran together for a while.

The next section of the race brought tree stumps, rocks, and other obstacles, and being a bit heavier, the other runner had more trouble navigating that patch than I did, so I pulled away and kept going. Now I had to make this mine. I had to give it my all. I started pushing through the increasing pain and fatigue. I walked, I ran, I walked, I ran through the swamps, water, mud… and in about eight hours, I crossed the finish line. I'd won!

Crossing the finish line gave me a huge sense of satisfaction. Not just finishing, but proving to myself I was able to accomplish what I set out to do—not just finish, but WIN.

It was clear now the spark was ignited, and I was committed to pursuing this path.

The very next month, I signed up for the PALM100 in Fort Lauderdale. I ended up winning that one, too, and setting the course record. The month after that, I ran another race in Northern Florida and won that one as well. My confidence grew, and I knew what I had to do.

Ultras, at the time, offered me a way of living an adventure. Karnazes' book had answered a lot of questions, but it was living that experience in all its rawness that made me truly appreciate it. The Keys took place on a road, whereas the Everglades and other races were in wild landscapes, and for me, that was something extraordinary. Something completely new.

Like most of us, I'd always lived in "civilization." I'd never experienced Nature before. It felt like I was truly living the adventures I had desired to fill the deep void in my life while living in New York.

The ultra culture was a breath of fresh air. On one hand, America represented the dream of money and success, the world in which I'd been up to that point. On the other hand, there's the clandestine, underground feeling you find at ultra events.

Ultra is a discipline that goes under the radar of mass media coverage. Financially, it doesn't compare to major sports. And don't get me wrong, every sport is an amazing journey of the human body's ability. But I think there is something unique about the personal challenge of what your body experiences in conjunction with the exploration of the great outdoors in ultra. There is something I believe we all feel individually in Nature that allows us to have a different type of camaraderie.

I loved this philosophy, this approach to sport. In fact, I noticed that at the finish line of ultras, people cheer as if *everyone* is a champion, from the first finisher to the very last.

It's a completely different attitude from what we are used to. The message I got (and that enthralled me) was that we're *all* capable of extraordinary things. We are all, potentially, heroes.

Or we can become our own heroes, at least.

The American ultra culture completely fascinated me because it isn't about competition. It went way beyond that. It was about personal integrity. Going beyond your own limits. Anyone can be successful. The challenge with the ultra begins within, and you just need to reach for the boundaries of your own self.

I loved those early ultra races. Someone counted down from ten and then…GO! We'd set off from a starting line drawn with chalk on the ground, and we ran and ran and ran for hours until we were exhausted and broken. When we finally crossed the finish line at the end, all we got was a slap on the back. Congratulations! No medals, no trophy. At most, a belt buckle and a goodbye.

However, the awareness of having crossed that distant finish line stays with you. It's like a flame burning constantly inside of you that keeps you going through everything else in life—you are now resilient, and you don't need anything else to make you feel fulfilled.

There was an innocence to it, almost like a feeling of pioneering, that made me fall in love with them.

In many ultras, it's not unusual for the top runners to stay on after the finish to hug all the other finishers. Finishing such a hard journey, and a hug is awesome because there's human connection—a strong bond established by what we went through, what we endured out there.

Obviously, whoever gets to the finish line first gets some kind of recognition for that result. But that's not the main goal. The goal is the journey itself. Whether you're the fastest or the slowest, we both have crossed the same terrain, we both have overcome the same difficulties to reach this goal that we had set for ourselves. Period.

Simple concepts. Which nonetheless removes that mean-spirited competitiveness you find in other races. It's more like a party where everybody's invited: old and young, experts and novices. Maybe it's like a new form of the pilgrimages of the past.

Humans have always discovered themselves while venturing into the unknown. We step outside the security of the castle, of our village, and go out to confront the world. We set off on a voyage.

When I was a kid in school, I did track and field because it was the only type of running I knew. When you see running races on TV, they are always in a stadium, like at the Olympics. I remember we used to go through Imperia, the closest big city near where I grew up, and there was a track there. It was so big, so majestic, I imagined what it felt like to be an Olympian. That's where I started running, until the strict training schedule and overwhelming pressure from the coaches began to take the poetry out of it. If you're a kid, you have to enjoy what you do. You have to play—you can't be wrung out as if you're at a job.

You need to develop not only the physical aspect but also the force to drive you. So, I gave up on running altogether, not knowing there were other kinds of running out there. Now, my eyes have opened to a new world that exists outside the stadiums and big cities, far from the track and asphalt streets, to trails that take you over sheer drops, rising and falling over majestic mountains.

That spring, after having done well in a few races, I got interested in the "Raid du Cro-Magnon." For starters, I liked the name. It's a mountain race that sets off in Italy and passes through areas where human skeletal remains dating back to Paleolithic times were found: the Cro-Magnon indeed. It was one of the oldest ultra-trails in Europe with a stunning course that starts in the Italian Alps, passes through France, and finishes on a beach in Monte Carlo.

I shouldn't have been allowed to enter. In fact, to be accepted to the Cro-Magnon, you need to meet certain requirements, which include experience in the high mountains, which I, living in Florida, obviously didn't have.

"I'll try it anyway." And I wrote to the race director.

"Dear Sir: Look, I've run a few races. I'm only starting out, but I have a burning passion…"

I told him how I adored those places in the Alps and how when I was a kid, my whole family would wake up with excitement at six in the morning to go skiing all day long. I was practically raised on those slopes.

He wrote back to me. "If you want to try and you feel ready for it, I'll accept you."

And just like that, I was in!

When I started preparing for the Cro-Magnon in 2012, I lived in a thirty-six-story building on the beach. There were, alas, no mountains for training nearby, so instead, I took the emergency stairs every morning for two hours, up and down, up and down, up and down.

But running in the mountains at altitude isn't just about knowing how to run uphill and downhill. It's a matter of hemoglobin, which determines the amount of oxygen carried in your body. My body wasn't acclimated to altitude or these dramatic elevation changes.

From the beginning, I kept up with the lead group. The first climb was five thousand feet, straight out of the gate.

"Man, how can they keep going like that?" I wonder, watching the others disappear up the steep trails. The steeper it gets, the more I fall behind. But I keep pushing. Then, from right behind me, a lopsided old man pops up, walking briskly as he passes me. It's Marco Olmo, the great ultra trail champion! Meanwhile, I'm suffering like a dog. I'm used to land that's flat as a pancake, and here I am running one of the most grueling mountain races in Europe with over twenty-one thousand feet of elevation spread over seventy-five miles. I was shattered.

I did the last twenty miles with the woman who was in second place at the time, and we pushed each other to keep the rhythm. As we approached the finish line, she started falling behind and kindly turned to me and said, "Go ahead, you go for it!"

"No," I replied. "We've come this far together, let's finish together!"

We arrived hand in hand, tied for twelfth place overall.

The first few runners had come in two or three hours ahead of us, but still, I couldn't be happier. I'd finished.

The Cro-Magnon made me rediscover the Alps—the trails, the snow and backcountry, the run in its most beautiful and primordial form, like it was for a Paleolithic man.

I was already passionate about ultra, but putting the two together, running and Nature…that was the crowning vision.

25.

RUNNING IS LIKE FLYING

When we stop using our bodies, we lose our verve, our spirit.

In the beginning, humans were perfect athletes, like many animals. A bird never stops flying, so why do we stop running? Our modern lifestyles have us spending all day sitting in front of a desk, then at a table, then in a car, after which we lie down in bed. In fact, our lifestyles have driven us to become so sedentary that we have forgotten our true state of being.

I often argue: What kind of life is that? Sitting all day, moving the tips of your fingers at most?! That whole concept is wrong, in my opinion. We're becoming more and more like the mass-farmed chickens we eat.

It's not just about looking better…our bodies literally deteriorate if we stop using them. That's how we get disorders and illnesses and massive depression in our society. We're like the little bird that spends all day in the cage. After a while, it gets fat and weak and in the end, no longer knows how to fly. But if you're the bird who goes out every day, flaps its wings, pecks at things, and struggles with the worm to pull it out of the ground, you're active—you move and you fly.

When we stop using our bodies, we lose our verve, our spirit. Even today, there are populations like the Tarahumara in Mexico in which even the old people run. And they aren't the only example.

I always considered Marco Olmo to be an absolute legend, not just because he won some of the toughest races in the world, but because he was almost sixty when he achieved those incredible results. He's a man who has continued to run his entire life. Not all of us are born to win, but we're all born to move. At all ages. All the time.

Running is a way to stay active and young. You see, children run, and when they run, they laugh. Walking is less of a thrill. You have to move so your heart is beating, thumping with a bit of zest. Little birds know how to walk on the ground, too, but when they are able to fly, they take flight!

You see, running is a bit like flying.

26.

FASHION VICTIM

SUMMER, 2012

The first step to becoming is to will it.

—MOTHER TERESA

It was apparent to me that Florida was not the right place for us. Perhaps it was the urge to be back among the mountains, perhaps it was the need to get away from too many painful memories. Perhaps it was both.

"I'm done. I'm outta here! I'm not staying here anymore," I said at last. "Let's go see Los Angeles; let's go check out California."

So, after just a few months living in Florida, Lauren and I left. "We'll go visit LA for a few days and see how it is. If we don't like it, we'll look somewhere else."

The second day we were there, we found a nice apartment,

and in a snap, we packed our things and moved to LA. We've been there ever since, and we love it. California's Nature is amazing, with a great diversity of environments that are accessible all year round.

Changing places is easy but reinventing yourself requires more time and effort. I continued to do some modeling because it allowed me to pay the bills. But it had become a drag. I was hungrier and hungrier for new experiences. I tried to keep a foot in each world, but the more I looked like an athlete, the less work I got as a model. From 185 pounds of muscle, I tried to get down to 150 pounds of lean power. Big arms, pectorals, and abs only get in the way. A long-distance runner needs long, tapered muscles—strong but not swollen. I had to choose which path to take.

Should I take the leap and become an athlete? What will I live on, then?

Unless you're playing in the "major leagues," you don't see much money in sports. In fact, many top ultra athletes to date still work other jobs to support themselves. It's never easy to abandon the old path for a new one. It was quite a daunting thought.

Then came the moment I was called to do what would be my last fashion photo shoot. Oddly enough, it was for a huge chain of running apparel in Germany. Big pictures of me running appeared on all the billboards in their stores. Even some of my model friends sent me photos. "Look, you're in Hamburg, Berlin, Munich, Dresden. I went to buy some shoes and saw you there!"

Finally, my conscience took over, and I decided to follow my passion and pursue running wholeheartedly. I was convinced that I could embrace that lifestyle and make it a career.

How could I leave such a glossy and high-paying world? I often argued with myself. The transition from fashion to running was a huge leap to take in the dark. And all odds were against me. If you look at it just from the financial point of view, mine was definitely not the wisest of choices. Definitely not a smart move.

27.

MY BODY, MY TEMPLE

You need dedication and patience before achieving any results because they don't come easy… It's like building blocks, one on top of the other, to get higher and higher. You're doing something important—you're building your temple.

One thing I adore is connecting with my breath, *aahh-huuhh-aahh-huuhh…* When you run, your heart beats faster. It's so powerful, and it makes you feel alive! You don't know what you're missing until you allow yourself to fully experience it and feel that sensation. And sadly, many people may never experience it at all.

Moving and sweating also serve to release endorphins. That's why when you come back from a run or have done some activity outdoors in the sun, you feel good and at peace with yourself.

I'd even say that it's awesome to get dirty in the mud or

fall and maybe even to cut yourself a little until you see a few drops of blood. That's me, that's who I am inside. That's how my body works. And boy, does it work well! In a few hours, the wound is already closed, and in a few days, it completely disappears.

The body is meant to be active. We're not supposed to try and preserve it. No, the body needs to be used, not mummified while we're still alive. The body isn't a machine; it's so much more. You have to use it because the more you look to preserve it, the more it deteriorates, weakens, and rots.

It's a question of physiology: if you don't move your body, the cells will receive less oxygen, causing acidosis, and an acidic environment leads to disorders. Whereas, the more you use your body, the more energy flows and the stronger it gets.

Move. Life is short. Act NOW. Go!!

When you find yourself alone with your thoughts and feel the regular cadence of your steps hitting the trail, those are magic moments of pure freedom. You're not happy about anything in particular—you're happy because you're happy to be fully alive in the moment. That sensation is a priceless privilege we can all access. That's probably the biggest motivation that pushes me to run enormous distances.

As time went by and I slowly progressed, I got to the point where I did training sessions of up to fifty miles at a time. One day, I left the house before dawn, ran through Griffith Park, down the San Fernando Valley, crossed the whole thing, went to the top of Verdugo, then back down the mountain. I crossed Hollywood, Beverly Hills, then ran back along Wilshire

Boulevard toward home near Silver Lake. Seven hours. At times, the route could take longer in a car because of all the traffic!

I tend to prefer running in Nature, clearly, but running can also be a good way to explore the city. Los Angeles is a giant metropolis, and I know it like the back of my hand because I've literally run across the whole city. Several times.

The training sessions are something you need to enjoy. While putting on your running shoes, you can't think, "Oh shit, I have to train." On the contrary, when you train, you need to be happy you're doing something you love, "I *get to* train!"

If you start with this concept in your head, it's no longer something you have to do. Rather, it's something you get to do—it's a pleasure. Like a surfer who dives into the ocean, you're going out there to play and do what you love to do.

Running works your whole body: arms, shoulders, torso, abs, lumbar muscles, glutes. When you're running, everything works in unison because you have to stand straight and maintain a good posture and the arms sway back and forth. Most often, I find the road to be monotonous and mechanical, but if you run on trails, the body doesn't repeat the same movement because it alternates between flat stretches and up and down hills, and even the level of effort constantly changes.

Running downhill is fun, like dancing. It's important to have a solid center of gravity because you have to stay upright as you go down, as if you're floating. Your legs move quickly to catch the next step while your arms stay at your side to keep your balance. You have total freedom of movement. In running, there's no theory. You don't follow a system or a master who says a movement needs to be done a certain way. You simply follow your innate nature.

Moment by moment, you adapt to what comes at you. Even on the most technical trails, you jump in and find the next step. You jump from one rock to another or dodge a branch. You run in the present when heading downhill; you don't think about it. There's no time. If you think, you've already thought too much. You've already lost a step, then you've lost two, and on the third one, you trip. You just have to go; that's the beauty of it. For me, that kind of run, simple and wild, is the most fascinating thing there is.

Preparing for a race is much harder than just running. There's a lot to learn from the process of training, how to deal with stress and also how to rest. You need dedication and patience before achieving any results because they don't come easy. Obviously. It's like building blocks, one on top of the other, to get higher and higher. You're doing something important—you're building your temple.

Imagine creating waves in a still pond. You have to push, then you let go, then push a little more, then you let up. And you keep pushing harder and harder to create an increasingly bigger wave. You push: stress. You let up: rest. There's a mechanism you need to understand: always progressively pushing a bit more, you create an increasingly better version of yourself. But the timing is fundamental. The skill lies in arriving at the top of the wave of your optimal physical condition right before the race.

To get to that level of fitness, though, you need to put lots of pieces of the puzzle together. It's not enough to take care of the physical part and look like a war machine. You need to put it all together: nutrition, stretching, massage, core exercises, and spending time outdoors to get used to good and bad weather. Everything together creates harmony. You don't just train your legs. I consider the combination of all these things to be an art.

Training is constant research, constant apprenticeship, a constant process of improvement. Every year, I discover something new. It's extraordinary because you realize there are no limits to what you can envision and achieve. I feel like I have yet to find out how far I can actually go. I still have great potential ahead of me, and that's *so* exciting!

In sports, you often hear, "That guy is thirty; he's old." Old?! We're just beginning to get into top form. And here's where physical maturity begins. The average age of someone who wins an ultra is between thirty and fifty. When I came in second at Angeles Crest, for example, I was thirty, the third-place guy was twenty-eight, and the first-place guy was forty-eight. The oldest guy won. It hits home. Because the further you go in life, the more you mature. You might lose a little speed, but you gain wisdom and patience. You learn to know your body and listen to it. And endurance increases with age. It's a psychological question. What is it that you endure when running like this? Severe discomfort. So, the better you know yourself, the better you manage yourself, and the more endurance you have.

I started doing yoga when Lauren and I moved to Los

Angeles. In the beginning, I used it to stretch and work out some tightness due to constant running and overuse. By doing yoga, though, I got a better and better understanding of how my body works. Because when you put yourself in certain positions and when you twist a certain way, you feel where it's pulling, stretching, opening up. You explore every part of your physical body with its blood and breath and consciousness. And the more you do it, the more you get in tune with your body until you radiate well-being. Now, I get up every day and do an hour of yoga. I've been doing it regularly, and I haven't had any injuries or problems ever since.

With practice, I've discovered that there's much more to yoga than I had thought. Initially, it was purely a physical exercise for stretching, then it naturally brought me to explore meditation.

It's amazing what the mind allows you to do. The body has limits, that's obvious, but a strong mind can keep you going even when the body says you can't handle any more. In fact, there's a saying: when you think you're at the end of your forces, you're only halfway. In my opinion that's not true: you've only just begun. Now, when I train, I basically meditate. Meditation is a practice that helped me become a better runner.

The ultimate goal is completeness, the union of the two forces summarized in the Latin proverb *Mens sana in corpore sano* (a healthy mind in a healthy body). Why aspire to less? Why develop only one of the two?

Don't neglect your temple. But don't forget about the consciousness that inhabits it.

28.

THE WOLF OF THE YUKON

It's hard to express because these are feelings we don't know. Or rather, feelings we used to know and have forgotten. They were the daily feelings of our ancestors, from whom we've drifted away.

It was the end of 2015 as I started to poke my nose into extreme adventures and expeditions. I was taken in by the pioneers of Polar exploration, the Iditarod in Alaska, and the Yukon Quest in Canada's Northern Territories.

The idea to put myself in extreme experiences quickly became an obsession after the UltraMilano-Sanremo (which you'll learn more about shortly). I wanted to run through Antarctica and cross the Sahara, the Atacama, and the Gobi deserts. I wanted to do all these things, and I wanted to do them on foot. But I couldn't just take off to the Poles, which are sixty degrees below zero, without any experience. If you want to do polar exploration, you'd better not just wing it. So, that's how the idea came to me of completing the Yukon Arctic Ultra (YAU), considered the coldest and hardest race in the world. I wanted to do it to put myself to the test and understand what it really meant to go "into the wild."

There's a white ribbon of snow and ice that goes from Fairbanks, Alaska, to Whitehorse, Canada: the Yukon Quest Trail. More than one hundred years ago, during the gold rush described in Jack London's novels, this trail linked the territories of the North and was used for communication and supplies. Some years ago, it was transformed into an extreme and exhausting course for a dogsled race. And in 2003, the YAU was born.

Before a race, I like to be alone, and that's due to the fact that I can't have anyone talking to me about their worries and concerns. I have to be aware of only myself—sometimes, even their encouragement is distracting. And, perhaps selfishly, that's all it is.

You have to push yourself to an elevated state that's almost unreachable in daily life in which you detach from the external distractions and arrive at an image of yourself that's not polluted. Pure. In which you are you. Centered, present, and confident.

All the rest is of no use to you. Then, you set off and do what you have to do: get to the finish line.

The days before the start of that race, we had to attend and pass a required training camp in which all the participants were brought into the woods and had to show they could start a fire in the snow, mount a tent quickly, and so on. If you didn't pass the test, you weren't allowed to start. The race basically takes place without any support, so each participant has to drag a sled behind them tied around their waist with a cord. The sled is full of all the supplies for sustenance and emergency.

In the other races, as extreme as they can be, every six to eight miles, there's a checkpoint or a shelter where someone helps you fill water pouches or gives you something to chew. Not in the Yukon. Out of one hundred miles, there are only two checkpoints: one at twenty-five miles in and the other at sixty miles. Then, nothing until the finish. And there's no one between one checkpoint and the next.

Passing through the hotel lobby before the start, I saw a small group of Italians speaking among themselves, exchanging advice. Some of them seemed to have had quite a bit of experience under their belts. They'd done the Yukon or similar exploits before. So, my father came up behind me, "Hey, maybe they're right, you should also…"

I looked at him and said, "If you want to stay with me, you have to understand I'm not interested in whatever they have to say. It's not important!" At times before a race, I could, and can still be, a bit tense. That's because *I* needed to keep my mind quiet. Because if I'm not quiet, I can't listen to myself. So, I picked up my things and left.

I have to stay in an isolated environment with myself. It's simple.

If you're not capable of living with yourself, within your mind, how can you expect to endure such a challenge? Once, a runner who was just starting out asked me, "How do you run for so many hours? I get bored after ten minutes alone. I don't know what to think about anymore."

It reminded me of the poignant response of a painter who had been asked a similar question: "Ah, my friend," he said, "that depends on who you are alone with."

It may sound weird, but when I'm alone, I talk to myself out loud. Outside, there might be nothing happening, but I'm inside my head, and I'm talking and listening to myself. In any case, when you're in Nature, you are never alone. There aren't any other people, but there's a connection with the Earth, and you can sense it. There's a connection with the other life forms that inhabit it. We're all part of the same entity. Everything is alive. Even though plants don't speak like we do, even though they aren't human beings, they're still *living* beings, and they have inner life.

Can you imagine? The starting line of the Yukon Arctic Ultra. There we are—runners, Nordic skiers, and mountain bikers—all ready to conquer, just under the polar circle, where nothing grows, barely any life at all. It's the middle of winter because obviously an extreme race takes place not just in a location that's very cold but during the coldest period of the year.

The race starts at ten in the morning. The first rays of the sun are barely poking into the sky. In the beginning, you run on the surface of a frozen river that winds through a canyon and infinite stretches of abyss. You pass by lakes, even frozen ones, then you hop onto a white trail entering a forest full of very tall fir trees. After a little while, I find myself alone.

Here in the Yukon, you lift your gaze and realize there is

nothing in sight but the most uncontaminated Nature you have ever seen. No utility poles, no roads, no houses. You're far away from civilization. And the more you lose yourself in this world, the more you get in contact with yourself. They say if you don't lose yourself, you can't find yourself.

I get to the first checkpoint. I fill my pouches and thermos with water and take off again. Around four in the afternoon, night falls. The temperature drops precipitously. During the day, we were at a comfortable twenty degrees below, but now, it's dropping to forty below. It's bitter cold. The world in front of me appears only through a cone of light emanating from my headlamp. Hours pass. This is a real adventure. This is exactly what I was looking for!

There's no one else I can lean on. Now, whatever happens, I'm completely responsible for myself. But I'm serene with everything, as I don't need anything. I feel great. If by chance something happens and I hurt myself, I'll die here. That feeling is strong, and it's something you rarely taste. You'll die *for real*. But that's where you feel strong because you're aware of yourself. In that moment, you know you're the master of your destiny.

That's the kind of experience I was seeking. That's exploration. Like when you find yourself in the middle of the Pacific Ocean in a rowboat. If you fall ill, they might be fishing your skeleton three years later as it drifts ashore in Ecuador. Who knows? I've never experienced this sensation so intensely. I'm here with myself in one of the most inhospitable environments on the planet! "You must stay alert." I love that kind of intensity.

Here, on a Yukon night, I have to keep running just to keep my body warm. If I stop for a few minutes, I'll die of exposure. They'll pick me up in the spring when the snow melts. Rather than scaring me, I actually enjoy knowing this. It's a form of power. I have to drink and stay hydrated. I have to eat well and maintain a stable body temperature. Each step is important, every step needs to be precise.

I'm not the only one to seek out these races. There are many marines or members of special forces who come to do them. They're not all professional runners, and they're not all necessarily fast, but they do extreme things to put themselves in situations of complete self-reliance. Because this is how you live truly extraordinary moments—moments that less than 0.5 percent of the population could ever experience. In fact, people come back year after year seeking that thrill.

You see, an ultra is already extreme on its own. If, in addition, you do it in an extreme place, then you're in an extreme situation multiplied. An ultra within an ultra. Not only do you bring your body to its limits, but you do it in untamed and rugged Nature. Not everyone has the desire to toe the line of survival. It's rare to live such intense moments in modern life because comforts distance us; they numb us and distract us from discovering this higher state. Most of us don't know these states even exist.

These races allow you to live extreme and unique sensations, to know yourself and understand how far you can go. This, for me, is pure discovery: not just a discovery of territory, but an inner conquest. And when you push yourself to that level, you feel as if you're seeing your essence. And yes, you want to win—but it's so much more than that. You're just looking to reach Ultra—to go beyond your limits.

You're not looking to be something. You realize that you already are.

* * *

West of here, in Alaska, Chris McCandless of *Into the Wild* wound up dying in the carcass of an abandoned bus in the middle of the woods because he no longer wanted to be part of society. He'd left everything, burned through whatever he had, and probed into the wild lands. I liked the book, and I liked the film even more. I also feel the uniqueness of these areas that are among the purest of our planet. Because here, there's nothing! These days, you can also go on safaris, but by now, the animals are almost fenced in, kept for our own entertainment or to appear as "extras" in National Geographic documentaries. Our last frontiers might be in the great deserts, the oceans, and the Poles. The rest of the world is nearly all "civilized." In the Yukon, though, there are only little bubbles of civilization amid the wilderness and imposing Nature, magnificent and cruel… Although it isn't really cruel. It's just harsh in that corner of the world.

After the second checkpoint sixty miles in, where I fill up my thermos with water, I find myself with about forty more miles of snowy ground to cover in the middle of the night. There's no one in sight. I look in any direction, and

I realize in that area around the polar ice caps for hundreds if not thousands of miles, I won't encounter a single sign of civilization. Endless valleys, rows of mountain ranges in the far distance, frozen rivers, and interminable forests. Low brush, white expanses up to the horizon. It's the difference between being in the ocean and in a pool. In a pool, you know there is always the edge if you need to rest. The experience is entirely different when you venture out into the ocean and get lost. This, for me, is what the Yukon represents. The opportunity to get lost.

I proceed in the dark, with my headlamp opening a visual field a few meters in front of my steps. This is my world. Imagine running for hours and hours in silence at the same relentless rhythm, feet sinking into the snow with every step.

You look up and see the stars sparkling, the Milky Way cutting the sky in two. You look down and see the footprints of animals, small and large: foxes, elks, animals you don't know. At times, you even hear sounds. Hours and hours and hours, always alone. That's you there, in contact with this Nature. It's hard to express because these are feelings we don't know. Or rather, feelings we used to know and have forgotten. They were the daily feelings of our ancestors, from whom we've drifted away.

At one point, out of the blue, I hear a rustle, and two silhouettes dart out in front of me then hop into the brush on the opposite side. Right behind them, another. This one, though, stays fixed right in the middle of the trail. A thick coat of fur, a fat tail, and two big yellow eyes stare right at me.

I stop, paralyzed. It's my spirit animal. It's the wolf. And it must be about ten yards away. Around us, there is only darkness and silence. The sled hits against my ankles.

And now?

Seconds go by, which seem like hours. There, I feel the power of Nature. I look at him, and he, through those yellow eyes, looks back at me. I have no control over the situation. My knife is hidden away in my sled. Suddenly, the wolf turns and proceeds on its way.

That was the most intense encounter I've ever had. More intense than with any deer, the various rattlesnakes, the mountain lion, and even the big bear. The wolf is, for me, the most fascinating of all animals. It was a moment with a meaning all its own, with an almost mystical value. If I close my eyes, I can still see him. I carry him with me. He's always there in all his might.

In many ways, we've evolved like wolves in packs, which makes it easy for us to identify with this regal animal—there's an innate synergy between us. I feel respect for this gorgeous and resilient being that has managed to adapt to the harshness of its environment. Not to subjugate it, but to live it in its fullness.

The cheetah is certainly the fastest and is the one-hundred-meter sprinter of the animal world. But if there was a totem for the ultra runner, a being that represents endurance, patience, and the ability to cross enormous distances in the most inhospitable places on the planet, then it would undoubtedly be the wolf.

After I take off again, for a long while, I keep looking behind me to make sure he isn't following me.

Onward. I have to keep moving. If I stand still without the necessary layers of protection, I'll freeze. In the sled, I have a heavier outer layer, like a parka. If I decide to stop and build a fire, eat something warm, or take a little nap, I have that option, too. The procedure to follow in case of emergency is relatively simple: immediately put on the parka, then take out the tent as quickly as possible along with the fifty-degree-rated sleeping bag. Get into the bag, press the SOS button on the GPS tracker, and stay there until help arrives. But since this area is very remote, it could mean waiting for several hours.

I don't stop. I feel a drive within me that could knock down walls. It's not a question of pushing. Rather, I'm getting pulled toward something, a calling. A matter of attraction. At the psychological level, if you push, push, push, after a while, you burn out. But if you're attracted by what you're doing, then it's not even an effort. And I feel pulled—I'm flying on that silent strip of snow.

But during those very cold hours of the night, a serious problem cropped up: my water reserve froze solid. I filled a thermos at the last checkpoint a few hours earlier. Since then, the temperature continued to drop: below thirty, thirty-five, forty. And in the end, even the water thermos transformed into a block of ice. There are still five or six hours until the finish, and I have nothing to drink.

If you wind up in a difficult situation, you have to manage to control your mind and emotions and not get taken in by panic. When I can't stand it anymore, I throw a few handfuls of snow in my mouth. "Better than nothing," I tell myself. But it's worse. You should never eat snow because in order to assimilate it, you have to burn energy. And then it makes you cold inside. You should first melt it with fire. But there's no time. I'm charging forward and don't plan on stopping. "Maybe I'm risking too much, but I'm running it all in one go. I'll recover when I get to the finish line."

It's still dark when I cross an enormous frozen lake and see the aurora borealis dancing above me, its fluorescent green illuminating my path. I get to the other side, and I should almost be there...But it seems like there's no end in sight. There's a lot of fog. I can't see very well, then all of a sudden, I hear a strange yell.

"Yi-ha!! Yiii-haaa!!!

It's my father, who just saw my headlamp and is beginning to celebrate. I follow his cheers and then begin to see, very faintly, the light of the lodge's beacon: the finish line. That lonely outpost in Braeburn. There's no one outside, apart from my father. It's a muted arrival. No applause. The doctor and the cook are holed up inside. The race director hasn't arrived yet, and the finish line banner hasn't gone up yet, either.

I have to knock on the door. "Hey, guys, I'm here!"

"Aaaahhh...There you are!"

"Yup."

It's eight in the morning. Still dark. Given the nature of the course and the fact that it had snowed the days before the race, I finished the hundred miles well before the cross-country skiers and even before the first cyclist. My father takes a picture of me before diving in the shelter, seeking warmth from the frigid temperature. I have a beard of ice and red eyes because my corneas are frozen. I stagger into the bathroom, and as I wash my face with warm water, I start crying. I release the stress, the emotions, everything. I feel safe.

Silence.

After I change and put on dry clothes, I have the station manager, a man with a long beard and arguable hygiene, make some scrambled eggs for me. Then, after I'm inside the lodge amid the blinding white, the first cyclist arrives. A German. As soon as he gets there, we hug, congratulate each other, and he tells me he camped out on the side of the trail for half an hour in the middle of the night because he couldn't stand the gelid wind blowing at him. On a bicycle, your legs move, but the torso is still, so he suffered more than I did. I must have passed him in a moment where I wasn't very lucid, without even seeing him. In fact, I thought he had already arrived.

After him, there came a French girl. But she came neither running nor by bike. She was picked up by a snowmobile. They brought her inside, undressed her, covered her, warmed her up, and took off her shoes. There was a thick silence in the room. Eight toes were black. Completely black. "They're going to cut off her whole foot," I thought. She started having bad issues during the night and sent out an SOS. Between grimaces of pain, she told me how she'd gone into her sleeping bag in the tent and waited four and a half hours for someone to come get her. Then, it took another four hours by snowmobile to bring her to the Braeburn station.

Frostbite hurts like fire. I had three little frostbites on my feet, and they burned like hell. I could only imagine what she was feeling.

I ran for twenty-one hours through the frozen Yukon. Six hours of light and fifteen of darkness. The second-place runner came, I believe, seven hours after me. I went full throttle with my head down. I clearly paid for it because I suffered immensely. The cold burns your inner fibers, the trachea, the stomach, and lungs. It cuts you down. I hurt for months afterward. But I can say that the Yukon went well, after all. I did this for myself because I wanted to see that part of the world and travel through it without worrying about the competition. You set off and manage yourself, and if you manage yourself the best way you can, then maybe in the end, you finish ahead. I had my material, studied it the right way, risked what I needed to risk, and it worked. Races go how they go.

It was my greatest adventure up to that point. Something I'll never forget.

29.

CRAWLING THROUGH THE VALLEY OF DEATH

JULY, 2016

Ninety percent of ultra running is mental, the other 10 percent is in your head.

—ANONYMOUS

At that point, my goal was to finish the two most extreme races in the world. I had done the Yukon, the coldest; now within six months, I was aiming for Badwater, the hottest. Against the cold, you can cover up as much as you want, but in hot weather, there's a limit to how much you can undress. When the temperature gets to be nearly 130 degrees Fahrenheit, you can do what you want, but the heat will beat you down. But I liked the idea of being challenged in those two extremes.

The original Badwater challenge was to go from the lowest point in the United States in Death Valley, California, to the highest (with the exception of Alaska), the summit of Mount Whitney, which I was well acquainted with after a storm had caught me up there. The modern race, due to the usual permit problems, stops about eleven miles before the summit on the slopes of Whitney. Notwithstanding that little discount, the Badwater Ultramarathon still offers, on top of its blazing heat, the beauty of not just of one hundred miles, like the Keys or the Yukon, but of 135, with two mountain ranges to cross in the middle. In short, Badwater is a long and grueling race.

The Badwater experience began that day in mid-February of 2016. I'd just come back from the Yukon, and that very morning, I'd received the letter of acceptance to Badwater. Only a hundred runners are chosen every year. With that letter, I had a shot of crowning another dream.

So, after recovering from the Yukon for a few months, I started to train for Badwater, which required totally different preparation. For the Yukon, I trained on trails during the winter at an elevation of ten thousand feet to find snow and temperatures well below freezing. While for Badwater, I had to do countless miles on asphalt—this one would be on the road—under the midday California sun with winter clothes, a wool hat, a K-Way wind jacket, long tight pants, gloves, and all the rest followed by 1,500 sit-ups at a time in the sauna to get ready for the high temperatures. Or I'd drag a tire with a rope around my waist through the streets of Los Angeles, with all the traffic stopping to watch me pass by. For three months, I prepared for the test, paying attention to the tiniest details from every possible angle. I did strength training, yoga, meditation, and I felt in top condition. I was lean and strong with ripped abs and tight skin. I was ready to run.

The moment comes when you're aware of being in peak condition, of having brought your body to the extreme to do extraordinary things. I could feel it: OK, the transformation has come. You did months and months of training to get here.

It's like preparing for a big party. And the race is the celebration.

* * *

There are a few seconds left until eleven in the evening when I look at my orange GPS and notice it's 117 degrees. Even after sunset, the temperature in those parts of the world is frightening. The usual countdown and…Go! We're off. We start out fast, but I'm relaxed. I'm immersed in the situation; I'm pushing but without feeling it; I'm dipping in the danger zone. There's a group of four of us in the lead.

Five years earlier, when I read my first book on ultras, Dean Karnazes described Badwater as the hardest foot race out there, the toughest challenge. He himself didn't even finish it the first time. They had to carry him off. As a matter of fact, most of the competitors don't finish on their first try. After that book, when I was still a beginner, I ran next to Pam Reed, who had become a legend because she had won Badwater. And now, I'm in that race. I'm thrilled and feel privileged to be in the elite group. Badwater always had this enormous allure. Badwater is Badwater—it's a thirty-year story decorated with champions. I feel psyched!

The dryness is overwhelming. A hot wind parches my throat, and considering the high temperatures even at night, every mile or two I have to refill the water bottle. For this reason, every runner needs to be followed by a support team in a car with all the provisions as well as technical and emergency equipment. There are a lot of cases of heat stroke, fainting, and runners collapsing on the side of the road.

The support team's task is to leapfrog their runner, park on the side of the road, get out with the water spray to cool down their body temperature, fill the water bottles, and give the runner food if necessary. They do this all while moving then get back into the car and repeat the process for 135 miles until the end. Given the extreme nature of the course, I have two support teams following me, alternating and switching duties halfway through. The first is made up of my father and three Italian friends. The second has Ashley and Brian, two of my dearest friends as well as very experienced ultramarathoners from California.

Around fourteen miles in, I run out of water, and suddenly, I can't find my team. Other teams pass by, riding alongside their runner, but I still don't see mine. At the seventeen-mile mark, we get to the first checkpoint at Furnace Creek. The lead group is pretty compact, and we're all there, moving. I've been out of water for three miles already. At this checkpoint, though, they only measure the running time and have neither drink nor food, as per the rules of Badwater. One's own team members are the only people permitted to distribute food and water to the runners since it's such a grueling race and everything needs to be calculated for each runner. Did I mention my throat is totally parched? It's now burning.

The volunteers at the station point out a group of support cars and vans up ahead, so I go off into the darkness of the desert, hopeful. I slow the pace a little because I'm a bit incoherent and I'm starting to cramp up. And that's when I realize: I've gone less than twenty miles, and I'm already seriously dehydrated. I have another 115 to go…

I finally reach the group of cars. It's the dead of night, and I point my headlamp toward them, hoping to recognize someone. There are no traces of my team. I continue, but I'm getting more and more discouraged. I've been running for almost six miles with my water bottle empty. I'm getting the dry heaves from dehydration, the cramps are more and more debilitating, and my head hurts. My lucidity is waning. Water here is an absolute necessity for survival. It's not called Death Valley for nothing. In training, under normal conditions, I can manage twenty to twenty-five miles without drinking a drop. But here in the desert, it's another story entirely.

Shit! I can't see anybody. Three quarters of an hour in Death Valley without water at 120 degrees. One. Hundred. And. Twenty. Degrees. And it's nighttime. Saying it seems a little crazy. I've never felt anything like it. I've been in the Sahara in Morocco, in Egypt, in Tunisia, but never anywhere like this. The air is hot, everything is always dry, drier, and still drier. You can't even manage to sweat because it all evaporates the moment it arises.

This kind of heat is hard to fathom if you think about it.

It's almost fascinating. But without water, it only means death. There isn't even a tree where you can get some shade. A cactus? Down here in the valley, you don't even see cacti. There's nothing. Nothing, and...nothing. Sand and rocks? Those volcanic rocks burned billions of years ago. It's a monstrous Nature. The vastness of these lifeless expanses is impressive, leaving you speechless and in absolute awe.

And I'm running right in the middle of it.

I'm staggering. There, it looks like them...Someone's handing me a water bottle. As I reach out to grab it, the bottle isn't there. Nor is the person. It's like I've entered another dimension.

I know these dirty tricks. I know them well. The mind does that. It pretty much happens during all the hardest ultras: you have a few hallucinations. You're running, your head is bouncing up and down...They're not vivid images, but you live them, you feel them. They're almost fun. One guy told me that during an ultra trail in the mountains, he'd glimpsed people working on their computers. In the woods. At night. And dragons hiding between the trees. When he got to the checkpoint, the doctor pulled him aside. "This guy isn't going anywhere!" He cut his bracelet and stopped his race. Rightly so. He hadn't even put on a jacket, and it was pouring rain outside.

You get hallucinations due to the fatigue and stress of having spent hours pushing. I've had visions of animals, people, objects that weren't there. In one of my first trail races, I ran and ran and ran. It was pitch dark, raining, cold, and when I was almost at the finish, I heard noises. I became paranoid about being alone in the woods. I went ahead but continued to hear noises, and when I turned around, I saw nothing. Maybe it was someone catching up to me? But what if it was some sort of predator? I went into panic mode. I felt like I was being followed. So, I stopped and picked up some rocks to protect myself against an animal attack. But it was nothing. It was all in my head.

After nearly an hour, one of my crew's friendly faces pops up out of the dark, running toward me.

"Where the heck have you been?!" He shouts at me.

He says they lost sight of me during the night. At the Furnace Creek checkpoint, they wouldn't let them park, and…I'm perplexed. I'm incoherent and can't quite catch what happened. Not that it mattered at that point. I ask them to open the door of our van so I can lie down in the back seat for a minute, rehydrate, and get some energy back with the hope of setting off again with a new spirit. I can't let a mishap and a couple of missed water bottles wipe out this whole experience. I feel like a deflated balloon, and it takes me more than fifteen minutes to get back up again. That's when the tailspin starts. You see, in these races, given the distance and adverse temperature, it's all about trying to limit the inevitable physical damage. But if after twenty miles, you're already in the red zone, it's a ditch that's hard to climb out of.

I somehow do and continue as my team and I had planned.

Mile ninety. With dawn and the beginning of a new day, I can see my second team. My Italian friend Daniele decides to tag along with the "California Crew," and I get my spirits up again. I start pushing a little more, trotting at a good click, and slowly begin to pass a few people. I get to the fourth checkpoint, Darwin, and discover I'm among the top ten. Exactly seventeen hours have passed. Slower than expected, but considering all the initial problems, it's not too bad.

This is where I had planned to make a move to close the gap and shoot for the podium. Instead, what happens? Exactly the opposite. Less than three miles after Darwin, I feel shooting pains in my lower back around my kidneys. I don't think much of it. Then I realize it's been fifteen hours since I last peed! So, concerned, I start drinking as much as I can. Finally, I feel the urge and pull off to the side of the road. The coppery red liquid that comes out of me is so disturbing, Daniele is petrified. I'm literally pissing blood.

I start to feel worried. Kidneys, stomach, everything hurts. These are the moments that define us. At that point, it's a question of understanding how not to give up and how to possibly find a way to continue. I need to find the motivation to move another step. Only one. One at a time. But shortly after a hundred miles, with more than thirty-five to go, I break down completely. Strong pains keep me from even walking. I'm having trouble eating, drinking. I'm having trouble staying alive.

My body is screaming for mercy, and I'm fading. I am close to throwing in the towel, but Ashley and Brian, who are seasoned ultra runners and have finished many tough events, won't let me abandon my dream. That's what the support team has to do in those critical moments. They're always there, every step of the way, to encourage me. Lauren, who's my wife now and drove straight from LA that very night, pops out of the dark and comes up to me. "Don't give up. You know you'll regret it."

The drama of the moment almost turns into comedy. We walk on the long white strip on the side of the road during the middle of the second night, through burnt valleys that seem to repeat themselves into infinity like an old video game. Gusts of searing wind carry mouthfuls of sand that get stuck between our teeth. It's so totally absurd that at times, we burst out laughing. I want to see how far I can take it at this point.

OK, I won't be winning. And it's not the adventure I wanted to have, but it's still an adventure, after all. That's the philosophy of ultras I liked from the very beginning: don't give up—just reach the finish line.

As long as I can stand, I can keep moving forward. The other competitors don't count. It's a personal challenge. This is where you come to know yourself. It's not all about winning.

Many times, I fall on my knees and get back up. I cross in and out of consciousness. It's by far the biggest fight of my life.

I have to finish at all costs. I'd learned so much since the Keys 100. I'd pushed myself to the limit in every race from the Yukon to the UltraMilano-Sanremo. I was truly going to reach my "Ultra" in this race, and I knew what it would take to cross the finish line.

From that point on, for thirty-five miles, it's a death march.

I practically drag myself like a tortoise, and despite all odds, the morning of the second day, I finish. Ten hours longer than I'd set for myself. But I cross that finish line.

It was a terrifying debacle. Terrifying. Borderline madness. "Enough, this is too much!" I felt like Chuck Wepner going up against Muhammad Ali. Chuck Wepner was the real "Rocky Balboa." *Rocky* was inspired by the true story of when the great heavyweight boxing champion, Muhammad Ali, in a publicity stunt, gave the opportunity for a no-name fighter to challenge him. They chose Chuck Wepner, an unknown Irish American boxer. He was tall, blonde, and quite ugly to say the truth. You wouldn't have given him the time of day. In the film, Rocky trains like a madman, wakes up at dawn to drink raw eggs, goes to a meat locker to punch frozen sides of beef, then jumps into the ring to confront the Champ.

This guy, Chuck, stepped into the ring and became an icon. Muhammad Ali was hopping mad because even though he kept pounding him, thrashing him for fifteen rounds, he just couldn't knock him down. Just like in the movie. That's the real story of *Rocky*. It's a kind of modern fairytale in which a poor underdog from the slums goes up against a kind of Goliath— this monster, this perfect machine, this super athlete champion of the world. He gets beaten to a bloody pulp, obviously, and loses. But he doesn't go down. He stays on his feet.

That's how Badwater was for me.

We slept through the next day. In the evening, we got a burrito and a couple of beers at the Mexican restaurant in Lone Pine. My old friend Daniele and I talked for hours that night as he came to thank me "for giving him a new perspective on life, for opening new horizons." This might actually be one of the most touching things anyone's ever said to me. He studied photography, but he's not a professional photographer yet. He aspires to become one. It will be a process of growth. If you don't give up, you keep getting better, step by step. You learn the art, and it becomes yours.

We're all on a path of development. And we each follow what we believe. We can all lead an intentional life that is truly worth living.

The next morning, when I got up, I had the strangest idea: "How about we go back?"

Daniele turned pale.

"I guess, if you want to go…let's go!" he said a couple of seconds later.

So after having run a 135-mile race, after having been horribly sick and pissing blood, we took off and ran, slowly, all the way back to the entrance of Death Valley. And this time, we really had fun—it wasn't for the competition, or for the buckle or the allure of it. It was for our own experience.

Simple. No prizes, no rankings, nobody else around. Just us, the desert, and the stars.

30.

MODERN GREEK HERO

When I run, I feel our ancestors, the heroes of antiquity running within me, encouraging me, inspiring me.

—Yiannis Kouros

Yiannis Kouros is the best ultra runner of all time. Period. His approach, to me, is more heroic than athletic. It's about absolute mental strength. Maybe it's no coincidence he's Greek.

When Kouros was a little kid, he wasn't accepted by his family, so he spent his time running outdoors. It gave him a sense of freedom. That's how he started, and soon, he discovered his talent. He liked long distances.

One day, he heard about the first edition of a new race called the Spartathlon. The Spartathlon wanted to retrace the real feat of the ancient messenger, Pheidippides, but not the twenty-six-odd miles from Marathon to Athens. They wanted to retrace the most daunting part of his original feat: the stretch from Athens all the way to Sparta: 153 miles.

Kouros was unheard of at the time, but he signed up. It was one of his first races. In 1983 at the base of the Acropolis, the race starts. Yannis sets off in the footsteps of Pheidippides. And he wins.

He ran the Spartathlon four times, and four times he won. To this day, no one has been able to beat his four records in that race. Kouros has also broken the world records in both time and distance: twelve hours, twenty-four hours, forty-eight hours, and six days. In six days, he ran a mind-boggling 639 miles! His record in twenty-four hours still holds after twenty years: 188 miles. That means he ran faster than seven minutes per mile for a whole day and a whole night. That's amazing!

To be clear, in a timed race, there's no preset finish line. The athletes start out on a circuit of a mile or on a normal track of four hundred meters, and they have exactly twenty-four hours at their disposal. Whoever runs more miles in that timeframe wins.

The toughest long-distance runners of the last twenty years haven't even come close to breaking his records. After one of his races, Kouros declared, "This record will hold for centuries." That's what he said when he finished. He was well aware of what he'd achieved. Because it wasn't just him; it's as if he became a channel for something much greater: the heroic quest. It was truly "Plus Ultra." He expressed this quest through running. But running was only a means.

Kouros had always been maniacal in his training. Obviously,

he had to hone his body to the extreme to bring him to that level. He was a machine. But he wasn't just that. "When I run," he said, "I run as if there is no tomorrow. Therefore, nobody can beat me. I am prepared to die."

Pretty amazing, isn't it? If you start with that mentality, you won't just be the one who vomits from the effort. No, you're the one who'd rather die than fail. But he's still alive. He's in his mid-sixties now.

Yiannis Kouros has nothing to do with running in Nature, or in the mountains, or on trails. He's strictly road and track. In the six-day race he did, they made him run on a track for eight hours in one direction then eight hours in the other to make sure he didn't wreck his ankles. He ran in circles for six days straight!

Though it's not the type of experience that enthralls me, I often get inspired by Kouros. Where the hell did he get that absolute mental strength?

He says he feels almost possessed, as if the spirits of the past were inside of him. "When I run, I feel our ancestors, the heroes of antiquity running within me, encouraging me, inspiring me." I don't think there's another athlete alive who can say this.

Even if his feet were destroyed, his knees blown up, his back in pain, and he was on the verge of losing his toenails—a pain that's worse than a toothache—he didn't care. He knew what he had to do, and he did it. The pain was there, but he forgets it. Imagine putting yourself in Pheidippides' shoes, charged with having to carry an extremely important message to the

Spartans. "Run as fast as you can; our fate is in your hands!" Imagine the anguish of the messenger who has to run from Athens to Sparta because the future of his people and his city depends on him. And that's exactly what Kouros imagined. He felt like the messenger, the hero.

It's curious how in modern ultra running, the toughest runner of all happens to be Greek. Almost as if, through his culture, he understood the essence of the hero.

Yiannis Kouros said his records would probably never be broken, but if one day it were to happen, they would be broken by an Asian—someone from China or Japan.

Why?

31.

THE WARRIOR MONK

We were Zen before we even knew what Zen was.
We're cool, we're relaxed, we know what we're doing.
And we wanna make sure we live a righteous life.

—Ivan Parasacco, Official Speaker of Tor Des Geants

An Indian monk by the name of Bodhidharma, so the story goes, around the year 500 AD set off on a long journey to bring Chan Buddhism to China. Arriving at Shaolin monastery, he began to teach not only the art of meditation (to make the mind stop) but also rigorous physical practices (to make the body move). Shaolin kung fu was born from this union of combat techniques with Buddhism's non-violent precepts.

For monks, who can easily fall asleep during long hours of meditation or the study of sacred texts, martial arts work like a blast of dynamite. They require inner discipline, keeping one's attention focused and alert. Martial arts, which, as the name implies, come from the art of killing, proved to be also extremely useful exercises for developing the spirit. Thus emerged the figure of the warrior monk, the complete human being who brings spirituality to the flesh and flesh to spirituality. For him, everything is sacred, and everything can be useful to further his personal growth.

From China, this form of Shaolin Buddhism spread to Japan, where it came to be called Zen. There, it had a profound impact on every aspect of Japanese culture, from the tea ceremony to haiku poetry all the way to the discipline of the samurai. Many samurai began to practice Zen meditation, not always for religious reasons but often quite simply to improve their combat skills.

Zen—incisive, rigorous, essential—avoids doctrinal teachings in favor of freedom from any preconceptions and always being fully present in the moment. The body is not an enemy or an obstacle to growth. Indeed, breath, posture, and movement become the very tools with which we root ourselves in the present. Zen is the act of uniting body and mind. Where the two become one, there is Zen.

This Zen wind that blew across Japan originally came from Chan Buddhism, which was developed in Shaolin monastery in China. It had arrived from India, where it was pronounced "dhyana." And dhyana means "meditation." Therefore, the root source of all these movements comes from the Asian discipline of cultivating and strengthening the mind. According to Yiannis Kouros, the discipline of meditation was absolutely essential for anyone who ever dreamed of challenging his records.

Meanwhile in China, in the period after the destruction of the southern Shaolin monastery, a pretty girl named Yim Wing Chun becomes the object of desire of the local warlord. He wants to force her to marry him. She rejects his advances, saying she would reconsider only if he succeeded in defeating her in combat. Shortly afterward, to her great fortune, the girl meets Ng Mui, a nun who's survived Shaolin, and asks if she will take her on as a disciple. The nun teaches the girl a new system of martial arts inspired by her observation of the fight between a snake and a crane. Armed with this technique, Yim Wing Chun defeats the warlord through this style of martial arts created by two women, which now bears her name.

Hong Kong, 1957. A notable master of the Wing Chun school, which emphasizes a relaxed bearing and the minimum use of brute force, accepts among his students a sixteen-year-old boy with a rather confrontational character who was born in America but shows a keen interest in the culture of his Chinese parents. The boy's charisma, dedication, and capacity to distill their essential quality would soon make Chinese martial arts famous throughout the world.

His name was Bruce Lee.

32.

ENTER THE DRAGON

If you spend too much time thinking about a thing, you'll never get it done.

—BRUCE LEE

Then, I discovered Bruce Lee. In my humble opinion, he was the consummate master. He embodied something greater, and to this day, I aspire to be like him. He wasn't just the most famous actor in martial arts films of all time, which is how most people know him. Bruce Lee was many things: he wrote notes that became books; he wrote screenplays; he was a director, poet, teacher and, notwithstanding his death at the young age of thirty-three, was also a lucid thinker. For me, a philosopher. In martial arts, he didn't settle for the pre-set path of getting a black belt. He was one of the few real researchers, someone who founded his own school. He didn't go around competing in order to win prizes, yet he taught people like

Chuck Norris, who was the world champion. He was the master of champions.

Bruce Lee was successful in everything he did. That's because he was no simple fighter. He understood what lay behind the martial arts. I've read many books, and as far as a mental approach is concerned, his *The Tao of the Dragon Warrior* is hands down the biggest psychological inspiration for what I do. His teaching transcends everything: sport, cinema, competition, victories. His concepts are closely tied to ancient China, but having studied philosophy in the United States, they are presented in the light of modern Western culture, a union that encompasses everything.

Bruce Lee applied himself with the same dedication, preparation, and abnegation to whatever he did. And he did it in an obsessive manner. To do great things, you have to be obsessed with what you do. Obsession isn't necessarily negative. You have to follow your passion—you have to exercise an absolute love in order to dedicate your whole being to a goal that requires such sacrifice.

There's a point in an ultra, after about seventy-five miles, or roughly twelve to fifteen hours of running without stopping, when the body of even the strongest person starts to fall apart. But in some races, you're not even halfway at this point. So, what do you do? At that point, it's no longer your body that's going—this is when your mind enters into play. Whoever has the strongest motivation wins.

So, what's the motivation for the strongest?

Running to come in first isn't enough—you're in such pain

that it isn't worth it. You're better off giving up and going home. If you do it for money, the suffering is too much; it's easier to earn the money some other way. And glory, the acclaim of others? At the end of an ultra, there isn't so much of that, either. So, what's the motivation for the strongest, capable of pushing you forward not just in the moments of crisis during a race but even during daily training for an entire lifetime?

Think about martial arts. If the aim of martial arts was really self-defense, today, it would simply be anachronistic, obsolete. What value does a martial art have in front of a man who is armed with a gun? Martial arts have survived to this day because in their highest form, they aim at a path of individual growth. They are a tool. Whoever understands them knows their ultimate goal isn't the defeat of their adversary. Before anything, the true warrior must defeat himself.

This philosophy and motivation can be applied to anything. The external results have no meaning. Sometimes there are results, sometimes there aren't. What counts is shooting a step higher: personal ascent.

This is what Bruce Lee said.

Once I understood this concept, it became nectar, fire. In the process of personal improvement, you aspire to be the best version of yourself.

Of course, it's hard. But when you take this path, it means every morning you have an inner strength that gets you up before dawn to go out and train and push your limits a little further. This gives you the vital lymph because you follow your dreams. It's simple.

If, on the other hand, you chase after the illusion of the good life and success, you'll never be happy because you'll only be looking for an image of perfection you can never reach. That's what creates stress, dissatisfaction, and, ultimately, depression.

There's a perfect image created by the media and the advertising world to which I used to belong. You see giant billboards with photos of young, beautiful, happy couples. But it's fake. First of all, they're not couples; those two probably didn't even know each other before the shoot. And if they lived together, they probably wouldn't be able to stand each other.

Faced with these images of utopian perfection, though, you feel insecure, crushed. Instead of looking to reach your true self, you're only looking to reach a projected image of what you think you should be. It's a concept that's really tormenting, especially for younger people. After a while, your courage wanes because you're not able to achieve it. And insecurity is an insidious feeling. You have to free yourself from that exterior image, believe in yourself, and continue on your own path.

It's all a matter of becoming what we want to be. When we don't find ourselves, we try to overcompensate for that void with substitutes like money, power, and popularity to reassure our thoughts.

Stories like that of Hercules are beautiful. He had to labor to reach his Mount Olympus and return to the gods, which was an expression of personal realization. They're all metaphors. But now, we've lost those metaphors, and everything has become a question of image. It's as true in fashion as in music and among actors and athletes alike. Many modern athletes exploit their physical ability only for money and fame. How many soccer players get bloated after they've finished playing? Think of Maradona. The body becomes a means for making money, but that's not the deepest sense of it. Our bodies are temples, which means we need to keep them up and dedicate time and love to them. Always. Don't let yourself go once the glory years are over. Don't do sports to make money but rather to be your best self. And don't stop taking care of yourself after you've stopped winning competitions.

Martial arts are an attractive path because you can do them throughout your entire life, constantly increasing your capacity. Unlike athletic performance, which always decreases after a certain age, they say in the martial arts you shine more with the passing of time. The older adept is generally better than the younger one. And that's how it should be.

In Asia, it's natural to think that development of the body leads to development of the mind. A complete person strives to have sovereignty over both. In fact, the ideal in Asia is neither the beautiful model nor the strapping athlete but rather the union of the sage and the warrior, a completely different figure. The archetype of the warrior monk, who unites mind and body.

Bruce Lee interests me more for his mentality than for his martial arts, which I've never practiced. His approach can be extended to any other field. You see, Bruce Lee isn't a warrior; he's an artist, a great man, a master. And not only in the martial arts. That's why his teachings have been so influential to me, for running and beyond.

Because in them, you learn the art of living.

33.

JOURNEY BEYOND

ITALY, 2013—THREE YEARS BEFORE THE YUKON

"You must be shapeless, formless,"
Bruce Lee tells me with a smile. "Be like water, my friend."

The Milano-Sanremo bicycle race has always intrigued me. I grew up there. I experienced it firsthand when it passed right in front of my house, practically at my feet. When I was little, my family lived in Arma di Taggia, in the center, right where the race passed through. So, together with my father, who was a huge cycling enthusiast, we were glued to the TV until the riders got to the town before ours, and then we ran downstairs to wait in the street and watch them whiz by—*zoommmm! zoommmm! zoommmm!*—right in front of us. They seemed like they were going a hundred miles an hour.

That race, the *"Classicissima,"* with its 175 miles, making it one of the longest races in the cycling championship, has always been like the soccer World Cup or the Olympic Games to me: a special event that only came once in a while. All that noise, the bicycles, the team cars, the TV, the helicopters, the motorcycles up front leading the way. It was an event, a glorious event that embodied the dream of many champions of our time. For me, it always had that unique fascination.

So, when I discovered ultras, one day I asked myself, "There's the Spartathlon in Greece, the Badwater in California, the Ultra Trail du Mont Blanc in France, this and that…But how come no one ever thought about running the Milano-Sanremo on foot?

Actually, the story goes way back, as the Milano-Sanremo didn't even originate as a cycling race. In 1905, it took off as an automobile race in two stages. The cars left Milan and stopped at Acqui, then continued the next day. But the first race was a flop because out of the thirty-two vehicles that started the race, only two arrived.

After that, the editor of *Gazzetta dello Sport*, seated at the Cafè Européen right in the heart of Sanremo, got the idea of launching the same challenge but by bike. The slogan was "Do you think it's possible to pedal from Milan to Sanremo without stopping?" And that was the foundation of something profound to spur the idea of overcoming human limits.

The first race was won by a French cyclist nicknamed "Le Petit-Breton," and from there, the splendid heritage that has become a thriving business with live TV and worldwide recognition was officially born.

In the summer of 2012, back in Sanremo, I met an old schoolmate, Riccardo, who I invited to our version of the Cafè Européen to introduce him to my idea: "Do you think it would be possible to run nonstop from Milan to Sanremo?" One century after the first Milano-Sanremo by car, then the ones by bicycle, the human spirit rears up to push its limits even further.

The UltraMilano-Sanremo may be Europe's longest non-stop foot race on the road. Even longer than Spartathlon. There are races in the world that are as long as one thousand kilometers, but with those distances, you have to stop to sleep. In the UltraMilano-Sanremo, by contrast, you have to run 175 miles in a time limit of forty-eight hours. That creates a condition where you can't sleep. You might be able to stop for five or ten minutes to grab a bite to eat, but then you've got to take off again. It would even challenge the limits of many experienced ultra runners.

To begin with, and perhaps a bit selfishly, I wanted to try and cover the course for the first time alone, to show it was doable. Not necessarily as a race but, ideally, as a charity campaign. Lots of miles to do good. I considered it a blessing to get an opportunity to run in order to raise funds for charity, and whoever has run even just a few miles with that aim knows how strong of a motivation it can be. We were going to raise funds for children suffering from neurological illnesses. You're not just running for yourself but for a greater cause.

We went to Italy and did a presentation for the fundraiser in a club in Milan, *Il Gattopardo*, and it was over the top. The following morning, I woke up with a fever of 104 degrees Fahrenheit! I had been on the national radio and did interviews here and there. That weekend, I should have run, but it was a disaster. I had a debilitating stomach virus for fifteen days and lost more than twenty pounds. I was already as thin as a rail, and by the end of it, I had no more legs. Just toothpicks. I was stuck in bed, as if I were in the hospital. That damned fever just wouldn't go away. It destroyed me. And, of course, with me, the run.

I had arrived at *Il Gattopardo* after months of practically living as a hermit. I had been completely dedicated to the training regimen and never went out or saw anyone. Then, right after the trip, with my immune system debilitated from exhaustion, I ended up in front of a splendid buffet. I got something to eat, and who knows, maybe I caught a bug from someone's spittle and it made me sick as a dog.

It was a fiasco. I'd put in months and months of preparation to get to that event. Thanks to the already glorious legacy of the course, we'd generated a lot of media interest, going on radio and TV and then...

It was just crushing.

All of that hard work with the best intent to raise money for charity and I couldn't even race? It was horrible, and I was beyond embarrassed. I hit a hard rock bottom right then.

Time heals, and the following year, in 2014, we said, "Let's do it again. I don't care what happened. We have a vision, and we're going ahead with it." You always have to go forward; you have to go past any initial setback. That year, we did it as a race. That was the spark. Riccardo and I began to set it all up. We put together a website and opened the registration. We launched the new challenge with a simple slogan: "*Do you think it's possible?*"

The response was overwhelming.

Fifty of the best runners in the world from more than twenty nations were selected. The Hungarian Szilvia Lubics, women's world champion in the twenty-four-hour run, would be there. So would João Oliveira, the Portuguese winner of Spartathlon and many other races. And then many Americans, Asians, Europeans, and the best Italians. Everyone loved the idea. It was the first edition of the foot race, and we had an international gathering of support for it from the best ultra runners in the world. National champions, twenty-four-hour champions, all ultramarathon winners.

It was surreal.

At the time, I had no resume to compare with the other participants. Yeah sure, I'd run a couple of hundred-milers, but I'd never gone any farther. One hundred and seventy-five miles was almost double my longest attempt, as I'd never pushed myself so far out.

I founded this race, I launched it, but I didn't want to sit back and just be the race director. I wanted to "live" this first edition, I wanted to run it.

"How do you intend to place?" I was asked.

"It's not in my control, but I guess finishing in the top ten would be a great achievement."

I didn't make much conversation. My mind was absorbed

by the enormous task ahead of me. I'd arrived in Italy two weeks prior. I met with the mayors and governors of the regions involved, made a presentation at the Sanremo City Hall, and held a press conference in Milan. I'd spoken with the Olympic champion marathoner Stefano Baldini, I was on the radio again and again, I did interviews with newspapers, and so on. Everyone helped us out. Everyone wanted to see this first edition of the UltraMilano-Sanremo on the same course as the famous *Classicissima* bicycle race. It was a new era with the possibility of further extending human limits, of giving the public a demonstration of what these bipeds are capable of. It was exciting.

We even managed to arrange for the mayor of Milan to marry a couple of American runners right in front of the Duomo cathedral and wish them good luck for the following morning, when they would both set off as husband and wife on this great challenge.

* * *

And here we are. Milan, March 29, 2014. I wake up at three in the morning. I have all my stuff ready to go, all laid out. I put on my compression socks, my shorts; I eat my two bananas and six almonds, per my habit, making sure to chew well, keep my legs raised, give myself a little massage, and get ready. We get into the car. My father drives. All my friends are there: Daniele; Denis, who will be my pacer; Emanuele; Paolo; and Luca.

It's five in the morning. It's still dark. We're near the Pavese canal, at the starting line, and we're ready. There's the Argentine, the Korean, the American, the Estonian, the German, the Frenchman, the Spaniard, and lots of Italians. The race director checks everyone in. There are journalists with their cameras, people with cellphones, and ambulances humming all around.

Ten, nine, eight—the countdown starts—three, two, one… Go!!!

And so, we're off.

We start pushing right out of the gate, keeping a pace of about seven minutes per mile, which is what you're supposed to keep at that level, I guess. Given the distance, that's running: if you start too fast, you risk burning yourself out, but after all that training, I got to the point where I could keep that rhythm up easily. João Oliveira, the Portuguese, pulls the group ahead of me. I'm right on his tail. Next to me is the "Other Italian" (a person I'd rather not mention), then I spot a Croat I know, a phenom at the twenty-four hours, and then a couple of other runners. There are six of us altogether, and we're moving at a good clip. Up ahead of us, there's an Austrian who took off like a train, then an American and a Korean who have already disappeared. Behind us, there's the platoon.

We run fast up to Pavia, where we enter the bike path that goes through a row of tall trees in the middle of a large plane. The sun is rising down there. It's spring, and all the colors are lighting up. If all goes well, the next day, when the sun rises again, I'll still be running.

We do a piece of road along Pavia's main boulevard, cutting through the city center, then come out from the other side. We cross Italy's biggest river, the Po, and go through the Lombardy countryside toward Piedmont. The landscape keeps changing softly. This is the first checkpoint. It means we're thirty miles in. About three hours and fifty minutes have passed. We still need to do about five times this distance. Better not to think about it. I let that thought go as I continue to stay behind the Portuguese, Oliveira. He and the Other Italian are without a doubt the two favorites.

At the start, I noticed the name on his bib: Oliveira. OK, it's him. Yellow shorts, white T-shirt, blue cap, and a little back-pack. He runs with his supplies. He's the one to mark. I run with him like I ran with Pam Reed in my first ultra. Oliveira is one of the toughest individuals I ever met—he came from the army. It seems a common trait, as it's not unusual to meet military people who are good at ultras. It's a mental discipline, after all. They come with another perspective: the objective is not to give up until the enemy has been annihilated, so if they manage to translate this approach into sport, they become unbeatable machines. Oliveira wins almost all of these long races thanks to his relentless resilience.

The person I love but didn't want at the start and didn't want on my team was my mother. That's because when she sees me in the races, she gives me that look full of pity. "*Oh my God!*" As if I were being crucified.

"No, mom, I *chose* to do this!"

And like any good mother, mine always has thoughts and worries, and in one way or another, her opinion is always that of a mother: a bomb in your head diverting you from your serenity, distracting you from what you're about to confront. I'd already told her I didn't want to see her.

Meanwhile, my team—my father and my friends in the black jeep—appear regularly along the racecourse. They bring me supplies, food, drinks, salt. I gave them a detailed timetable, minute by minute, of everything I would need. This time, I felt like I'd made a perfect plan. Fats, proteins, carbohydrates, and electrolytes in doses that were minutely studied and mathematically calculated. It was the first time I felt like I'd perfected the art of nutrition. I have to stay on my feet for many, many hours. During my other races, I went about it with approximations. I always tried to finish, but I often went through the wringer. I'd reach the end so devastated sometimes I couldn't even take off my shoes.

Oliveira, on the other hand, decided to come without his team. He has a backpack over his shoulders and uses the checkpoints to resupply. But whenever he needs water, the other teams along the way are happy to give it to him. He even comes to my team for things to eat. A banana here, honey there, peanuts, chocolate. You give a hand to everyone, and again, here shines the true beauty of the race, of the sport in its pure state. It's almost like running among friends—you create an atmosphere of respect and mutual support. Of course, if you run, you want to win, but you want to win while the others are giving their best, not because they fell or got sick. You want the others to give their best so you can give your best, too.

As the miles slowly pile up, I start to get fatigued, and Oliveira pulls away from me. Then I catch up, then he pulls ahead. And then again and again. After a while, he turns around and says, "C'mon, c'mon! You got this!" He wants me to keep up with him; he's trying to spur me. It's a gesture that surprises me in a way. He's the champion. I never would have expected such kind behavior. He's trying to push me to regain my strength so I can follow him.

I try to stay behind him, but I'm pushing too hard, so I decide to slow down while he keeps his pace and takes off. The Other Italian goes ahead with Oliveira while I let up a bit. A little later, I catch up to the Korean who started out strong, then I pass the Austrian who's already breaking down, and finally, I even catch the American. It's Dave Krupski, the runner I met during my second race in Florida, the one I ran with through the swamps with alligators. Now he's a good friend of mine, and between a smile and a cheer of support, we run the next forty miles together. We pass from the Lombard cities to the plains and rice fields.

By now, the two in front, Oliveira and the Other Italian, are nowhere in sight. At one point, Szonyi Ferenc materializes behind us, a Hungarian Ironman with whom we begin doing a little back and forth.

Then we get to the center of a small town, and that's where things go a little haywire. The biggest setback in the organization of this first run, of such a long race, is course marking. It's still in the pioneering stage, so Krupski, the Hungarian, and myself go left at a roundabout toward Novi when we're supposed to go right. We run and run, but after a mile, mile and a half, my father, Krupski's wife, and the Hungarian team look at the road book and realize we've taken the wrong road. Shit!

So, we immediately call the race director.

"Jump in the car," he says. "Go back to the traffic circle where you got lost. Get back and pick up the race from there."

These are his instructions. That's what's done in other long races, and it often happens, even in trail runs. At Badwater, they even give you a flagpole to stick in the ground if you feel bad. You can go wherever you want. You can go to sleep in a hotel, then go back, pick up the flagpole, and start again where you left off. So, the three of us are brought back to the traffic circle where we took the wrong turn, and we start again from there. We lose about ten, fifteen minutes at the most. We get to mile sixteen with Oliveira and the Other Italian ahead of us and a lead of about half an hour. We've been running for almost nine hours.

Krupski and I continue running together toward Ovada. The landscape changes again, and there are more hills. You can see mountains rising up at the horizon, beautiful colored vineyards, smaller villages, and medieval towns, as he and I start having an epic bonk. It happens to both of us, more or less at the same time, after one hundred kilometers. Krupski stops and pukes his guts out. I don't vomit, but I'm in pretty bad shape. I stop, too, and wait for him. I hold him up with my hand behind his back.

"Do you need anything to drink?"

Then his wife comes, my people come, and we give each other a hand. The Hungarian passes us. Shortly afterward, the first-place woman, Szilvia Lubics, passes us, too. Then another runner passes us, and then another. There's no getting around it. I'm hurting, and he's throwing up. We walk a piece together, then we try running again. We get to Ovada at mile seventy-five. We're in about ninth or tenth place. But what was it that Yiannis Kouros, the greatest of all, said? At sixty or seventy miles, you haven't gotten to the ultra yet. This is when the game begins.

I'm constantly looking to answer the Great Question that won't go away: "Why? Why are you doing this? Why do you have to suffer so much?" I feel dreadfully tired; my body is devastated. The nausea wells up from my stomach to my whole being. I try to muster up some courage: "Right now, everyone who's still in this race is battling their demons…" I start getting excruciating cramps in my stomach. I can't take it anymore. I'm thinking of stopping, of pulling out of the race.

At the exit from Ovada, I find my team's black jeep parked on the side of the road. I crash in the back seat. Krupski disappears into the car next to us. We both decide to stop for five minutes, at least. We're clearly on the verge of falling apart. We need to stop for a moment now because here's where the climb starts.

Meanwhile, two, three, four runners pass us.

"No, this won't do. I'm not even halfway through. I have to pull out."

Winning, at this point, is no longer a strong enough motivation to keep going. And money—which isn't there, but even if it was—isn't enough. Competition can't be the fuel, and it shouldn't be. You have to find within yourself the motivation that pushes you to go beyond. If you say "I want to win because then I'll get recognition," it's not a strong enough motivation. It's outside of yourself. And after fifteen hours, you'll start to break down. Whereas that's when the ultra hemerodrome wins: the runner who knows the answer to the Great Question.

Pheidippides. The messenger. He who is willing to sacrifice himself to bring the good news.

But I'm laid out right now in a car, and I can't continue.

"How the hell can I keep going?!"

My father looks at me with a worried frown and a super serious expression. Thank God my mother isn't here.

"What can I do now?" I feel so sick, my stomach aches, I have a pounding headache, my legs are throbbing, everything hurts.

"Try to eat this." Manu comes with a banana in hand.

I try to chew, but it's hard to swallow. I scratch my head, trying to find a way to pick myself up.

That's when my friend Denis shows up from behind the car. He pats my leg three times. "C'mon, that's enough!" he says. "Let's get up. Let's go!"

Denis is my pacer. According to the rules, after sixty miles, a runner can have someone run alongside for psychological and logistical support. After many hours of running, you're not very lucid. Denis is a strong runner and a good friend. He's younger and has no experience in ultras, although he was a great cyclist when he was younger. He's always had a tough mindset.

He understands the spirit needed to be shaken and pushed on.

Not eyes full of pity. "C'mon, let's walk to the end of this road!"

In a situation like this one, the positive energy your team members can transmit is absolutely fundamental. In the darkest moments, they are the ones who can turn things around. I force my stiff legs out of the car. Krupski sees me and joins me. This is where the Turchino climb begins.

"This'll be the end of me..."

Meditation. Don't think ahead. The fear of failure is what paralyzes. I'm not afraid of crashing; I'm not afraid of going for another hundred miles. "You must be shapeless, formless," Bruce Lee tells me with a smile. "Be like water, my friend."

Easy to say.

I don't think about what happened or what is going to happen. I just go. We'll see what happens later. Maybe I'll fall in ten strides and that will be the end of it. But at this moment, I'm completely present, involved, alive. This control is the meditative state. You don't think about anything else. If you learn this, when you find yourself in those terrible moments, with no more strength and pains everywhere, you can manage to find your serenity by breathing and meditation. You can find yourself, your center, your motivations.

In order to find yourself, you must lose yourself.

You only think about this precise moment. So, you act. Unbounded. You breathe. Breathe deeply. Slowly, I manage to unravel the tangle of thoughts. I'm like Peter Pan who has to keep his happy thoughts otherwise he won't be able to fly. Even in the worst times of a race, you have to maintain your positivity. So, I start walking, then trotting, and then I start running. Something miraculous happens. I get so high that Denis and

I hit the Turchino climb running as hard as we can, as if there is no tomorrow. We leave Dave behind us. I pass another six people going uphill. I'm so full of adrenaline and endorphins, I feel like I'm in seventh heaven. Like I can do anything. I run headfirst, and for a brief moment, I feel invincible.

Inside, my body is in a sorry state, but by now, it's as if I've detached myself. Ascetics get to this state through isolation and meditation, fakirs by lying on a bed of nails, samurai warriors by standing under an ice-cold waterfall. And ultramarathoners get there by running.

It's only by pushing the body beyond its maximum threshold of discomfort that you get to the state of complete presence. If there's no pain, you'll never get there.

Yet, it's by going beyond that you feel emancipated, elevated beyond all logic and certainty. It's there, right there, that you feel...like a hero.

You go so far beyond the state of total discomfort that you transcend yourself. I see myself, see my body down there running, *and I'm up here*! This is levitation. I run, and it happens in the middle of the race. The others can't see it, but I'm flying.

Why are you running? "Because running is like flying!"

The race is just a means, and here, during the UltraMilano-Sanremo, for the first time, I'm fully experiencing what this other thing is: *ultra*.

After so many hours of running, you should be dead, and yet, you're still running like a madman. I pass this one, pass the next one, catch up to the first woman, then the Hungarian guy, and get to the top of the Turchino, where there's a checkpoint. As I grab some quick refreshments—bananas and some almonds—all the people are cheering me on, and a friend comes up to me.

"Go, go, go! You're about to catch the front runner!"

"What do you mean? Catch who?" I must have at least two or three guys ahead of me.

But it seems that during the climb, I passed even the third-place runner, who was sitting in a car and I didn't see him. And Oliveira, the Portuguese soldier?

"Oliveira is sick. He stopped because of hypothermia, and he's in the back of the checkpoint, lying on a bench with covers on him."

So now I only have one runner in front of me. I'm in second place?!

I'm exhausted but on with the attack! It's wide open. With ninety miles already in my legs, I take off downhill to Genoa with full strides, running as fast as I can. I go so fast that at some points, my pacer can't even keep up.

The hunt has begun.

34.

HUNTER AND THE HUNTED

Now, I feel like the wolf.

I'm feeding off this rollercoaster of emotions. Rushes of adrenaline push me toward my objective—because yes, selfishly enough, I wanted to be the first one to do it. I give it everything I've got because I'm driven by that pure desire. I'm not running to win but to be the one who shows it is *possible*.

On the descent from Turchino, I have the whole Mediterranean Sea in front of me, and I turn hard right into the via Aurelia. I've got the Maritime Alps on one side and the sea hitting the beautiful coast on the other. I go through a few tunnels. In a short while I'll be in Arenzano, the checkpoint at one hundred miles. I've never gone farther than this distance. From here on out, it's completely unknown territory for my body. I've brought it to my previously known limits. From here, I go "plus ultra." And not just by a few miles. I've been running for fifteen and a half hours. That means four marathons in a row at a pace of three hours and fifty minutes each, with hills. And I have three more marathons to do before I finish.

It's overwhelming, but I try not to think about it.

In training, I'd never done anything remotely comparable to this. How could I? In training for this event, my longest run was fifty miles. Not any more than that, otherwise I would have risked burning myself out before the race.

I'm running like a madman. I get to Arenzano, and just as I'm entering the aid station, to my great surprise, I see the Other Italian walking out! He sees me. His jaw drops.

He's frozen still. He didn't expect me to be there already. And I also assumed he'd be far out in front. As he's leaving, I enter the checkpoint. I'm there for two or three minutes at the most. I take a sip of water, a handful of peanuts, but I don't want to stop.

"OK, I'm set." I thank the volunteers for being there. And before I know it, just as quickly as I walked in and announced myself at the checkpoint, *"Michele Graglia, Number 8,"* I'm saying, *"Thank you! Goodbye!"*

I'm off.

I don't see him. The Other Italian has disappeared already. I get back onto the road, but by now, I have him in my sights. Here, it's a new chapter. Everything changes. Everything. It's another story.

Now, I feel like my favorite animal—I feel like the wolf (though at this point, I have yet to encounter him in the Yukon). When I race, I never like to be in the lead. I prefer staying back and giving chase. I always have. It's just a mental game that gives you strength. It transforms you. In a race, it's nice to catch up to someone. Staying ahead is very intimidating and quite tiring, mentally. When I'm in the lead, I get anxious that someone is coming up behind me, and watching someone pass you is demoralizing. As an athlete, you have to learn to manage it.

So, from my perspective, I'm on the attack now. But I'm still experiencing a big crisis. I take off running, then I start feeling sick. I keep going forward, and still, I feel sick. But I keep going. He must be several minutes ahead of me. I get to a point where I see this vast expanse ahead of me, and he's not there.

"I have to pick up the pace," I tell myself.

In the meantime, I see his team's car, though despite my efforts, I start breaking down again, losing energy. I have to slow down and walk many times. I'm not well. I feel very tired. Nine, ten, eleven o'clock at night. We've been running since five in the morning. I woke up at three. I'm starting to get very sleepy.

I can see his team is still there, right next to mine. They hone in on us. There seems to be a scuffle going on between the two teams, my father and Daniele against two or three of the Other's. Usually, the different teams help each other out—after all, they've been on the road for almost twenty hours, too. But I notice they're having a discussion. When Denis catches up to run with me for a while, I ask, "What happened?"

"No, nothing. Don't worry."

They don't want to tell me anything that could take my mind off the task at hand. So, I keep going.

The Other Italian is just up ahead, but I can't manage to catch him because I keep slowing down. Worse, I'm falling asleep on the road. I remember little hills and tunnels, gulfs and coves. Savona, Spotorno, Varigotti. Sheer cliffs overlooking the sea and tranquil little beaches. And other tunnels cutting through the rock. But I'm on the Aurelia highway, which only has one lane. Cars are speeding past me. It's night. I fall asleep.

"Whoa, watch it!" A car's headlights brush by me, waking me up.

I run and run but my eyelids are becoming too heavy. I've been going for twenty hours. *Vrooom!* A truck passes. I slap myself, spray water on my face. I can't manage to stay awake. And yet, it's not like I didn't train for this, too—on many nights I tried not to sleep. I drink some Coke, but that doesn't work either.

"Look, I have to stop. Let me take a nice power nap, and then I'll be off again."

I lie down in my father's jeep. It's nice to have all my friends around me. These are the things that give pleasure. With the window open, I raise my swollen legs to drain some of the weight of the blood and lactic acid.

"Just twelve minutes, OK? Twelve."

I shut my eyes and I'm sleeping like a stone. *Boom!* I feel a hand shaking me.

"It's time."

"Uh, already? I have to go already? No!!"

Still, I get up.

Banana.

Coca-Cola.

OK, I'm good to go.

I get out of the car. My first steps are like those of a marionette, all skewed with stiff legs. I take off again.

I'm at mile 140 and change. I catch a second wind. I feel great. Finale Ligure. Another checkpoint.

"C'mon, he's close! He's having stomach problems, too," the volunteers tell me. "He's slowed down a lot."

Another rush of adrenalin. I'm psyched. He's not well. On with the attack!

It's still dark when I get to the bottom of the pass and start on the flat road that continues along the shore of the gulf. And in the distance, halfway down the straight road, I see a light. At first I'm not sure, but it's him. I can finally see him. I'm catching up.

I feel ill. I need music. I put on my headphones, and "Ten Feet Tall" comes on. A house music song full blast in my ears. I run and I feel like a giant. He's down there...we got him.

I bear down on him with my stride—*pum-pum-pum-pum-pum-pum*, and when I catch up to him, I lower the music, take off the headphones.

"C'mon buddy! Let's go; we're almost there."

He looks at me with a shy smirk and doesn't say a word.

I put the headphones back on and turn up the music. Good, now I have to run even faster. He's not well, and seeing me like that will shatter him. Basic psychology. A little head game is necessary at times. I pick up the pace. Pushing, pushing, pushing as hard as I can.

"He can still see me. Shit! He can still see me. I'm sure he can still see me…" I push. "There, a bend in the road. Aaahhh! C'mon!" I keep pushing and pushing. "C'mon! Up to that flag!" Got it. "Keep going till the next one." I get to the next one. "I'm hurting, I can't make it." "C'mon, c'mon, just a little more, down to that car! Now comes the bend." I turn into the bend. "OK, let's see." I turn once, turn twice, head into the curve.

"Now he can't see me anymore! Aaaahhhh!"

I slow down and walk a little. I'm doubled over. I need to drink, eat. I can't make it anymore. But I can't stop, otherwise he'll come up. So, I keep going. I keep going.

I've pushed too hard. My legs are falling apart now, I can't feel them anymore. "It might kill me, but this one has to be mine."

When you're experiencing something so hard and devastating, you can be as well-prepared as you want, but after running twenty plus hours straight, you're falling apart. Everyone's falling apart. It's inevitable. And again, that's where meditation comes in. Because it helps you to manage the moments in which the body is clearly no longer able—it's the mind that pushes you forward. *If you don't have a higher motivation than yourself, you can't keep going.*

That's why I'm ready to die in this race: because it's the first run. Because I created it. I'm writing my own page of history here. It's so meaningful to me that I'm ready to do anything to accomplish what I set out to do. It's one of the few moments I feel like Kouros.

I won't let go. I refuse to let go.

Who can possibly beat you when you're willing to risk everything?

Throughout history, there were always people who were willing to die for an ideal. That's how powerful motivation can be. It's motivation that makes you unbeatable.

Why do you do it? Certainly not to catch up to him, no, but to catch up to yourself as a human being. Not for glory that shines in others' eyes but for the glory within yourself. For that sense of personal actualization. That which no one can give you or can ever be taken away from you.

Human beings have to realize themselves. There's no greater goal, in my eyes. Each individual has to fulfill themself.

When I find out the Other Italian doubts my effort and has accused me of cheating, all I can think is "Easy to think, isn't it!? But you weren't there when I was waking up every morning before dawn…"

I said I would be happy to finish among the top ten, but I had trained to the peak of my capacity. I had prepared myself with total dedication and sacrifice like never before. I knew what I had to do, and I did it, without holding back. I never skipped a training session. I never deviated from my diet. Every evening, instead of partying, I went to bed early to rest my body and mind for the next day's workload. Every day, I pushed my limits a little further. Months and months of preparation. In training, I got to the point where I did more than a marathon a day. Thirty kilometers before breakfast and another twenty in the evening. Then on the weekend, I'd go for the long runs, maybe forty to fifty miles at a time. I did an absurd number of miles. All on roads with Yiannis Kouros on my mind.

I trained in the gym. I stretched and did yoga, hours of meditation, got massages, and did cryotherapy to help my muscles recover so I could start running again. I did everything I could.

"But you weren't there. You don't know what I had to go through to get to this point!"

Night ends and dawn arrives. The Other Italian, now in second place, is close behind me. The fiery ball of the sun rises behind me, and its rays give me another boost of life. The night is hard to get through because the body is used to sleeping, of course. The sun gives me new energy, almost as if I had slept. But everything is aching. Albenga: thirty-one miles to go. Alassio, then Laigueglia, Andora, San Bartolomeo, Diano Marina, then another big pass, Capo Berta, very steep. I get there in a state of oblivion.

At this point, I'm almost done. At this point, I'm in the lead. At this point, Sanremo is all that's on my mind.

35.

IF THERE'S A WILL, THERE'S A WAY

If you don't have a higher motivation than yourself, you can't keep going.

The UltraMilano-Sanremo, despite being on the road and in the middle of traffic, was the most profound ultra experience I'd ever lived up to that point. That's because it's the longest race I'd done to date. Here, I entered uncharted territory. Up until this day, I had never run more than a hundred miles. Doing seventy-five more after that sounds unreasonable. On paper, I know what I'm up against, but on a psychological level, I have no idea.

I go through moments in which my body experiences so much discomfort, I detach myself, and it seems to me, paradoxically, that I could run forever. Not much changes in twenty, twenty-five, thirty hours. And I want to see how far I can go.

I experiment on myself and observe that the body can do the truly extraordinary. If someone had told me a few years ago I would be running a marathon, I would have said, "Forget it! What's the point of the effort?" Now, I'm pushing myself to do seven in a row.

Pushing the body toward its limit, I feel pervaded by a powerful force. Like the fakir on his bed of nails, I transcend my body. But you don't get to that level easily; you reach it when you have to do a lot of work. It's a constant cycle of crisis resolution to reach euphoria. The longer the race goes on, the more often I get that sensation of euphoria, and each time it's stronger. But, the crises keep recurring. I have debilitating lows followed by exhilarating highs followed again by hard patches. You go up, then you plunge back down. The deeper the lows, the higher the highs. And the higher the highs, the deeper the lows. The cycle is both beautiful and overwhelming.

The pain is constant. It's not that you say, "I'll do a marathon. It's hard, but then it gets easier." No, it always progressively gets harder and harder. The body slows down because it accumulates tons of toxins. But what I learned is to try not to evade the discomfort; you have to go looking for it! Everyone is afraid of fatigue and pain. And yet, if you accept it and go through it, then it's no longer scary. It's an inevitable part of the journey, and if you do accept it, you find bliss.

It's not by chance that ultras are considered a metaphor for life because there are countless highs and lows. When there are lows, you get stronger, and when the beautiful moments come, you appreciate and savor them more because you made it through the hard ones. When you understand this cyclical nature, you manage to have more control over yourself and your life.

Nature teaches us that after the devastation, there's always rebirth.

In fact, that's where you see the true spirit of the ultra-marathoner—the one who manages to push when the others don't have anything to give anymore. That's why I consider ultra running an amazing practice, and the name shouldn't be attributed to runs of less than sixty miles. Because ultra means going beyond the physical. It's no longer a run. The marathon is a sport, but ultra running is a different discipline altogether.

The beauty of it is that after a certain point, it's no longer a physical performance at all. Absolutely not. In ultra, you set off to find the very fabric of your soul. That's why I consciously make that sacrifice, because it's the most profound experience. Of course, there's an absurd amount of sacrifice involved, but everyone has to sacrifice a little in life. And if you give a little bit of yourself and obtain results, imagine what can be accomplished when you give it your all.

After 140, 150, 160 miles, I start crying, bawling like a baby.

Real tears of joy. I would win the UltraMilano-Sanremo because I simply want to show that it can actually be done. For as much as ultra runners can be depicted as superheroes, I know I'm a very ordinary person. We're all alike. That's why I don't like the image of heroes, at all. Being a hero is like saying, *"Look at me! I'm better than you."*

No, no, please, let's break away from that pedestal. Let's

break away from wanting to overpower and diminish others. Maybe sometimes, you could just *feel* like a hero as you become your very own inspiration.

In my childhood, we were raised with the idea that someone becomes a champion because he or she was born that way—they were a special person. The gifted ones. They can, and you can't. They have what it takes, and you don't.

We looked at Olympic champions, and they almost seemed like abstract people. Unattainable examples blessed with God-given gifts. But I discovered throughout the process that's not how it is. If you convince yourself we are all equal and they've gotten to where they are because of hard work and complete dedication, then your whole life has a different meaning.

Nobody is special; no one is born a hero. The truth is that more often than not, dedication beats talent.

"And now I'm nearing Imperia," I say to myself, "and once I'm there, I'm home!"

I start the Capo Berta descent, and just when I get to Imperia, I see a group of people waiting: friends, supporters. They're all clapping. Then, despite my request, my mother's waiting for me. We share a powerful moment between us as she gives me a high five on the run.

People start gathering. There are forty, fifty bicycles riding around us, keeping us company for a while. There's a group of local runners cheering on my team and me. It's becoming a group journey to the finish, with everyone in unison. It's hard to believe.

I feel like I represent something at this point. I'm no

longer running for myself. And that's the special thing. At that moment, I'm not the one winning a race—I'm the one striving to reach a much bigger goal.

I realize it's not about winning. It's deeper than that. It's the same spirit that must have compelled the great adventurers and explorers to prove something—to leave a legacy, a mark on this world. It's the indelible sign of yourself. It shows you took part in the progress and the evolution and that you contributed to the evolutionary emancipation of our species. When you have a motivation that's so strong nobody can beat you, at that point, you're not running for yourself—you're fighting for your ideal.

The UltraMilano-Sanremo represented my legacy. My dream is for this race—which started with automobiles, then bicycles, and then a foot race—to continue for years to come. And who knows, if there's a little kid at the window who sees this race pass in front of his house, maybe he'll understand and get inspired, just like I did.

"Beyond human possibilities!"

There are no limits.

If there is a will, there's a way. What seems impossible is no longer impossible, if you work hard.

This is the vision.

Just as an explorer goes searching for it, a singer sings it, and a writer puts it into words, a runner runs it.

36.

HOME RUN

I realize it's not about winning. It's deeper than that. It's the same spirit that must have compelled the great adventurers and explorers to prove something—to leave a legacy, a mark on this world.

And so, I arrive in Imperia. Now, I'm home. I'm not interested in anything else but the finish line. I don't want to know who's behind me. I don't want to know what's happening or how; all I know is I just have to go. There are all these people cheering me on, following me, and there's the last stretch of coast, which is just stunning. At the exit of Porto Maurizio, we pass in front of the track that inspired me so much as a kid. In fact, I turn around and pay it homage, sending a thought of gratitude because my passion for running was born there and also died there. Or so I thought. That place had represented something at first but ended up ruining the spirit of the run.

Today, there is a rebirth of that special spirit—a reconciliation with the pleasure of running.

Then I leave the Aurelia and hop onto a road that cuts through San Lorenzo toward Sanremo, a road that winds along the coast with the sea just a step away. And there, in the late morning, I get to the beginning of the bicycle path and find a sea of people! Word had gotten out that a local guy was coming…The radio stations put out the news, and people filled the streets. They came out to wait for me. I can hardly contain the tears from pouring down my face.

The things our imagination can come up with, it's amazing. So many people…Everyone is eager to be part of my vision. It's so special. People on bikes, runners, old friends. People I haven't seen in a long time, people I didn't even know, everyone running along with me. When I stop, they stop, too.

At some point, I'm also hit by a deep sciatic inflammation that makes it hard for me to even plant my feet. So, I'm on the verge of falling apart completely. I stop, double over, try to recover, try to stretch a little to lengthen my fibers and feel a little less pain. Then I take off again. Then I do one or two more miles with everyone cheering, "Go! Go! Go!"

We get to Riva. I'm severely gassing out, but I say, "Alright, Riva…And then there's Arma di Taggia, my town. It's my hometown!"

I get all excited. It's full of people on the streets and on the bike path. Everyone is waiting to give me a high five. People— long, long groups of people. I get into town, and the town council's head of sports is there along with a friend of mine who is literally going crazy, shouting in the middle of the path when he sees me coming.

"I can't believe it!" he says to me. "Come here, come over this way…"

And instead of letting me go straight, he has me take a little detour, a little extra piece in the pedestrian part of the town as a tribute. Besides that, there's even my ninety-year-old grandmother, who has come out with her friends to spur me on.

It's a party.

I weep some more. Overwhelming emotions. I weep like a baby, right there.

Suffering and weeping are often seen as things to hide. We're too afraid of suffering; we always avoid it. But suffering makes us grow. It's useful. It helps us appreciate moments of beauty and helps us embrace happiness with open arms. If there's no effort and everything is given to you, or you always want immediate satisfaction, you then lose the flavor of things. You lose the pleasure of having them, making them, achieving them. If every-thing is always easy, you never truly appreciate anything at all.

I'd realized this when I was sitting on the windowsill of my fifteenth-floor apartment in the big city. You no longer appreciate anything, you despise people, you hate what you have because you can never get enough. Because what we're really looking for can only be found *beyond* things. When you *do something special*—digging, expanding yourself, liberating yourself, trying to push yourself beyond what you know—you live those incredible moments and everything becomes crystal clear.

I'm in Arma di Taggia. I see my grandmother, and I weep. I see friends and weep more, huge tears streaming from my face.

I still go between moments of euphoria to moments of despair. When I see someone, hear something, or a thought comes, it's like a key that allows me to go beyond—to go another kilometer, like an elevator that always goes one floor higher. Just when you say, "I've made it to the top!" there's another floor, and then another, and still another.

This is where I grew up. During the summer, we practically lived in Arma, always by the shores, always on the beach. I run through this place that's so full of meaning and memories for me. It's my home. I remember the cyclists whizzing by when I was a kid, when suddenly I notice...

The streets are full of children!

The staff and teachers let them out of school to cheer us on. I look around, and I also see my friend's parents and grandparents. People I know, old friends running with me, and people I haven't seen in ages pedaling in front of me.

These emotions give you fuel. I feel horrible, try to pull myself together, give myself inspiration to regain my pace and motivation, but with this rocket fuel, I feel like I can keep going forever. I want to get to Sanremo in this state of mind. Then I want to turn around, go all the way back to Milan, and relive it all over again.

As kids, we fantasize about a wild and reckless life, then most of us settle down inside a safe bubble where everything is comfortable, everything is easy and convenient.

If you don't push yourself to the utmost extreme, you don't

explore your realms. If you don't open your frontiers, you keep yourself from extraordinary experiences. That doesn't mean you have to go out and kill yourself running an ultra; it means finding something that allows you to get into real, unique, and incomparable contact with yourself.

37.

IN SPITE OF EVERYTHING

A man travels the world over in search of what he needs and returns home to find it.

—GEORGE MOORE

I keep pushing and pushing, and even after running almost thirty-two hours straight, I push some more. My whole team jumps out of the jeep. We're arriving in Sanremo. Even my mother joins us. Then, at the last stretch, the last few yards, they shout, "You go ahead!"

They're all arm in arm like a choir behind me as I cross the finish line. Arms raised. I take the flag that's been handed to me and drape it over my head, then double over and break down.

This moment is the crowning of a dream.

It's pure magic.

I can't stop crying. I've been weeping since the previous night. I'd stop for a while then start all over again, experiencing moments of glorious intensity. Laughing, crying, feeling joy, suffering. Everything. Literally everything.

I wanted to show people it was possible to finish this. Even if I wasn't really sure it was.

It's an ovation in Sanremo. Ranks of photographers, people crowding all around, other people pouring in, the town councilors, friends, interviewers...

Then, just like that, I hopped in the car, went home, and laid down in my childhood bed. I could finally sleep.

I lived the adventure I was seeking. I was an explorer. I walked among my ancestors on my path to Zen. I had even been prepared to die for it, but instead, I found my *plus ultra*.

I found myself.

38.

CHALLENGING THE GIANTS

—FOLCO TERZANI

RHÊMES-NOTRE-DAME, [VALLE D'AOSTA, ITALY], 2016

We're in a parking lot at the foot of a black giant whose head is lost in the fog. Small points of light blink up there, like desultory fireflies in the night. One of those lights should be Michele.

I imagine him, free, crossing mountains and valleys, alone with his thoughts. He's seen the orange sunset over the distant horizon, and now, he might be pulling on a warmer layer to prepare himself to enter the dark silent hours. I, too, would like to embark on a similar endeavor one day. For him, this is only the first of several nights because we're at the Tor des Géants, the "tour of the giants," one of the longest ultra trail races in the world. More than two hundred miles of rocky and technical high-mountain trails with about twenty Alpine peaks that go up and down. The elevation changes are insane. The mountains are the giants.

The first competitors will be busy for a minimum of three days and three nights, without sleeping if they can, battling against dragons and hallucinations and demons that will yell at them to stop. The others might take as long as a week. I'm part of Michele's team for the first time, together with his old friend Daniele; his father, who by now follows him all over the world; and even his mother, who is learning to maintain the implacable positivity you need for such an endeavor.

The lead runner came by a while ago. He ate something quickly and then took off again. But people are mumbling that he's pushing too hard. "You'll see, in a while, he'll crash." Meanwhile, two Spanish runners have arrived at the Rhêmes-Notre-Dame checkpoint: Oscar, who's already won the Tor three times, and his friend Julio. Now they're inside, eating something warm. I watch them discreetly from the window. They're joking between themselves, but Julio is starting to look pale. I may be wrong, but it does seem to me that Julio's face has a ghostly hue.

Two hours ago, the last time we saw him, Michele was looking good. His legs were moving. He wasn't in the lead, but he told us, "You can't run this race like the hare. You have to be the tortoise—an athletic tortoise! We're forty miles in, so weirdly enough, this is still only the beginning."

At 9:30 p.m., I feel the first drops of rain falling. Now, in addition to the fog and night, there's rain. We wait. We're not the only ones to wait for Michele. The newspapers billed him as one of the favorites, so spectators are curious to watch him pass by.

Michele is an hour and a half late. But now we can see two or three lights that have just come up from over the top of the big mountain and zigzagging down slowly.

His mother, though, has already started to lose her new-found detachment. "Something's wrong," she tells me. "I know his pace!"

I, on the other hand, think it's a tactic: stay back, then give chase, like the wolf.

It's 10:30 p.m., and Michele is still nowhere to be seen. Several runners who were behind him previously have now passed him. We start to worry. He's lost another hour in the last section. What's happened to him?

There is applause and cheers for the arrival of another runner at the checkpoint.

"Bravo!"

"C'mon, c'mon, c'mon!"

"I thought it was finally that Graglia guy," an older woman says, turning to the young man next to her. "But I read he used to be a model in New York…uh, this guy doesn't fit the bill."

The spectators giggle. A small, somewhat hunched over guy is just entering the checkpoint. Several more minutes pass, and from the dark veil of rain, a figure even more hunched over and shattered appears.

"Michele!" I yell.

He's limping, holding his arm stiff against his ribs. His clothes are caked with mud, and his right cheek is swollen as if someone's punched him. He disappears quietly into the checkpoint, where only his father is allowed to follow him. We stay outside, trying to figure out what's happened.

His mother just got news. She whispers to us, "The fog came down. Up on the mountain, you couldn't see anything. He'd just gotten over the top and started coming down when he didn't see a sharp turn. He went straight and literally stepped into the void. Thank God, Michele saved himself. He hit a rock…" She's visibly shaken. "It's dangerous up there. Last year, a Chinese runner died…"

"And what does he want to do?" I ask. "Continue?"

"We're men, we fall," his friend Daniele says stoically. "You don't run with your face. If they don't stop him for safety reasons, he ain't stoppin'!" He knows Michele.

"But it's still early. He's got three more days of running ahead of him, if not four, in these conditions!"

"So? That's the spirit of the ultra!" Daniele states.

"Damn…" I gasp.

In the meantime, other runners are coming into the checkpoint. The doctor is inside; she's checking him. His bruised ribs are the biggest problem. Luckily, there aren't any fractures, but Michele is having trouble breathing. Every time he inhales, he feels a stab of pain around his lungs. The doctor finally gives her professional advice: stop.

Shortly afterward, Michele emerges from the checkpoint. He wants to try and continue. The people around him clap. He clicks his headlamp back on and takes off slowly. He crosses a wooden bridge over the river then enters into a wood and disappears, scrambling up a rocky trail.

Fifteen minutes later, Papa Graglia's cell phone rings. Michele can't go on in his condition. He's dropping out.

That night, sprawled on the couch in the living room of the rented chalet, I can't sleep. I think of all the men and women who are still out there running in the mountains as day alternates with night with only a few shelters scattered here and there where they can rest.

At 8:30 in the morning, we're preparing breakfast. Michele's swollen cheek is turning purple. No point in pretending everything's alright.

"How do you feel?"

"I guess my ribs ache a bit."

Suddenly, tears well up in his eyes. And in mine too. "You fall on your face, you pick yourself up and keep going," he says. "There's no other way."

"But I know you did a lot of work to get here. Do you think you'll find another race?"

He shakes his head. "Now I have to start from scratch. The downside of our sport is that you can't say, like in soccer or motorcycle racing, 'OK, it wasn't my day, I'll get it next time, in a week or two.' I won't be running another race for at least six months. I have to lick my wounds now. I build sandcastles in preparation. The higher you build them, the more of a mess they make when they crumble. You get to a peak of fitness that you can't sustain for more than a couple of months, max.

Naturally. So, when you screw up a race, you can be sure you're going to be a little bitter because you feel like you've wasted months of training. But, hey, it can't always go your way."

Michele lets himself be tempted by a box of cereal that I bought for myself yesterday.

"I'm like a bear coming out of hibernation. I could eat everything!"

Indeed, I'd never seen him devour so much sugar. Usually, his discipline is ironclad.

"Oh, why not...Every once in a while," he laughs. "It's all gluttony, I know, but now I honestly don't care."

The TV drones in the background with some sort of talent show.

"Today, we'll make a big salad. And then for ten days, I don't want to do anything. Nothing. I don't want to run even one stride!"

"What if we went for a walk today?! You know, toward that place you showed us the other day..."

It doesn't occur to me to say, "Seeing as you just ran sixty miles yesterday and you even got beat up a bit, don't you think a day of rest would be in order?"

"You're on!" he says. "Let's head to the glacier. There are some beautiful lakes up there. C'mon, let's go!"

From the moment this free day popped up without having to run, without having to be part of a support team, and we just happen to be in the Valle d'Aosta surrounded by the splendor of the Alps, we decide there is no better way to spend it than by vagabonding up another mountain.

We decide to do something special today. We'll visit a glacier at the beginning of the Val Ferret, which melts into three streams, and we'll do it without even taking a trail. We'll just go straight up the mountain.

"By now, you must know," I say, taking off my shoes, "for me, going barefoot is essential. If you love the Earth, you want to feel her, touch her. When you're racing, you just might need shoes, but today is a day off."

It's a beautiful morning. The clouds have dispersed, the sun's out. Once we get past the first dense wood, where I nearly step on a viper, even Michele decides to take off his shoes.

"I'm going barefoot, too!"

The climb isn't easy, and it takes us several hours to go a few miles. But what does it matter? That's the beauty of it. Live, play, enjoy Nature in the simplest way. We get to the top of the alpine pasture, into the part of the meadow that separates the tree line from the steep rock face leading to the glaciers. We don't feel like pushing any farther, so we stop. Anyway, we've managed to make it up here, barefoot, to look at the world from above.

We sit down on a big rock by the stream. It's beautiful here, so we stay a while, with pleasure. I lie back and admire the reflection of an airplane floating on the river between two clouds. We hadn't thought to bring food with us. But I notice there are some blackberries next to our rock. And they're ripe! We eat a couple of handfuls and drink a few sips of ice-cold water that has just melted off the glacier.

The gurgle of the water, the whisper of the wind, the tall blades of grass swaying.

"You know, Michele, that fall of yours yesterday was perfect!" I say. "It was the move of a martial arts master. It brought us to something purer than victory."

"Right. The race was beautiful, but I was having trouble finding the will. That's never happened to me before. And then I wasn't expecting all that attention. I felt like I'd fallen right back into modeling. Back to that image, but the image of what?"

I do the voice of a play-by-play announcer: "After his triumph at the Yukon and his defeat at Badwater, he once again returns to first place!"

We laugh.

"Adversity saved us from an image of empty glamour and success," I say. "Think about how it would have been if after tomorrow morning, we were all at the finish line ringing bells, and then in comes Mickey Graglia, the triumphant winner. Everything according to script!"

"Yeah, I agree. This script's way better! I got to pick myself up again after the fall...This is way more interesting."

"You have to keep it simple. And we've had a beautiful day without pushing, in harmony with creation."

"Total peace."

"So, what's next? What do you want to do now? What do you have in mind? From the laps around the track when you were a kid to the five-mile runs with your model friends in New York to your first one-hundred-mile race, dramatically unfinished, up to the glory of the 175 miles of the UltraMilano-Sanremo, you leapt into the more than two hundred miles of Tor des Géants. Now what? Still longer and longer races? Where's the limit?

Silence. So I continue.

"You know, last night, I couldn't sleep. And then this idea hit me like a bolt of lightning. Instead of crossing another mountain chain or a desert or an entire country, why not run around the whole Earth?!"

"My God, Folco!" Michele's eyes light up, all excited. "You don't know this, but what you're saying closes a circle. That is, in fact, my biggest dream. When I was in New York, before even knowing anything about ultras, I read about a guy who'd gone on an entirely human-powered circumnavigation of the world. And I practically traced the route, country by country, city by city, street by street. I have it all mapped out! I'll show you. It's incredible."

"How much time would it take?"

"Thirteen years—I think that's what it took him. He did the oceans in a little rowboat and the land parts on a bike..."

"No, I wouldn't use wheels if I were you. You're a runner— you can cover those distances with your own two feet."

"For sure, that's even better! Awesome. Now *that's* a great project. A tour around the planet! I think I could do it in less time, as an athletic feat. I'd need a year maybe, or two, or three. Who knows?!"

"There are obviously some risks attached..."

"Obviously, but that's the fun part. Otherwise, it wouldn't be an adventure, would it? You don't know what you're up against. Hey, it's what we've always said: races are all well and fine, but for what? To *go beyond*. To discover the world, Nature, our own selves."

EPILOGUE

IN THE SUMMER OF 2018, MICHELE RETURNED TO THE starting line of the Badwater Ultramarathon, the race that had beaten him down to his knees and made him piss blood two years prior.

When the runners set off at night, the thermometer read 124 degrees Fahrenheit. When the sun came out the following day, temperatures rose to an infernal 130 degrees Fahrenheit, making it the hottest race in the history of the event.

Mickey kept running, never stopping, not for a single moment. When he finally reached the finish line some twenty-four hours later, he was welcomed by the race director and blinding flashes from all the photographers ready to capture the feat: he'd won! *Plus Ultra.*

ACKNOWLEDGEMENTS

I'D LIKE TO DEEPLY THANK EVERYONE WHO BELIEVED IN me and my vision, even when sometimes it didn't make any sense at all.

First of all, thank you to Dino Bonelli for being an outstanding mentor, confidant, and, most importantly, a true friend.

Thank you to Folco for his special friendship and to his savvy pen for initially sharing my story in *Vanity Fair*, an article that allowed us to delve into the depths of my journey and sparked the curiosity of Ester Mazzoni at *Sperling & Kupfer*, who gave us the opportunity to publish this book in Italy back in 2017.

A special note of appreciation goes to Phil Shawe for sharing the same passion and for offering the opportunity to confidently pursue my dreams, as well as to the amazing team at *TransPerfect* for their incredible support.

Thank you from the bottom of my heart to Miranda McGuire, who has now been by my side through many adventures. I'm forever indebted for all your monumental support and beyond grateful for the beautiful friendship we have created. Know the best is yet to come.

I'm immensely thankful to Audrey Birnbaum for her editing expertise and for her exceptional patience and guidance in adapting this book from its Italian version. A daunting task for sure. Without her, this book would most likely still be a tale for the bar.

Luca Mich, Matteo Demicheli, and the whole *La Sportiva* family. Your unparalleled support is priceless. Thank you deeply for sharing the same vision.

Dean Karnazes for showing me the way. His story, his book, his words not only changed my life, but they actually saved it. And for that, I will forever be grateful.

Last but most certainly not least, special thanks to my wife, Lauren, for always being by my side and for her unconditional love and extraordinary support throughout the years. She always inspired me to be better, and I couldn't imagine sharing my life journey with anyone else.

ABOUT THE AUTHOR

MICHELE GRAGLIA is a former top model and is currently one of the world's top ultra runners. Since 2011, he has competed in over thirty ultramarathons all over the world, often winning and setting course records.

He has set Guinness World Records for his runs across the Atacama and Gobi deserts. His wins in the Yukon Arctic Ultra, with temperatures below −40 degrees Fahrenheit, and the Badwater 135 in Death Valley, with highs above 130 degrees Fahrenheit, made him the first person in history to win both the hottest and coldest foot races on Earth.

Michele studied yoga and meditation in Rishikesh, India, and is an RYT-certified yoga instructor as well as a USATF-certified running coach and sports nutritionist. From 2016 to 2020, he was a yoga and mindfulness coach at the high-end Malibu retreat The Ashram.

His motivational speaking has inspired thousands around the world.

Today, he lives in Big Bear Lake, California, where he balances his life between ultra running and being a dedicated husband to his beautiful wife, Lauren.

FOLCO TERZANI is a writer. He was born in New York of European parents and grew up in Asia. After studying philosophy at Cambridge University and film directing at NYU, he made the last documentary on Mother Teresa of Calcutta, *Mother Teresa's First Love* (now on YouTube). His book with his journalist father Tiziano, *The End Is My Beginning*, became a million-copy best seller in Europe (not available in English) and was made into a film. In English, he recently published the fable for older children *The Dog, the Wolf and God*.

Made in the USA
Monee, IL
28 June 2021